Contents

How to get the best out of this book

Most chapters spread across four pages but some spread over two pages. All chapters focus on one topic and should help you to keep 'On track' and to 'Aim higher'.

Title: tells you the topic for the chapter.

What do you need to know? and **What will you learn?** tell you what you need to know before you start this chapter and what you are aiming to learn from this chapter.

Key facts: set out what you need to know and the ideas you need to understand fully.

Language: help to build up your mathematical vocabulary. Remember that some words mean one thing in everyday life and something more special in mathematics.

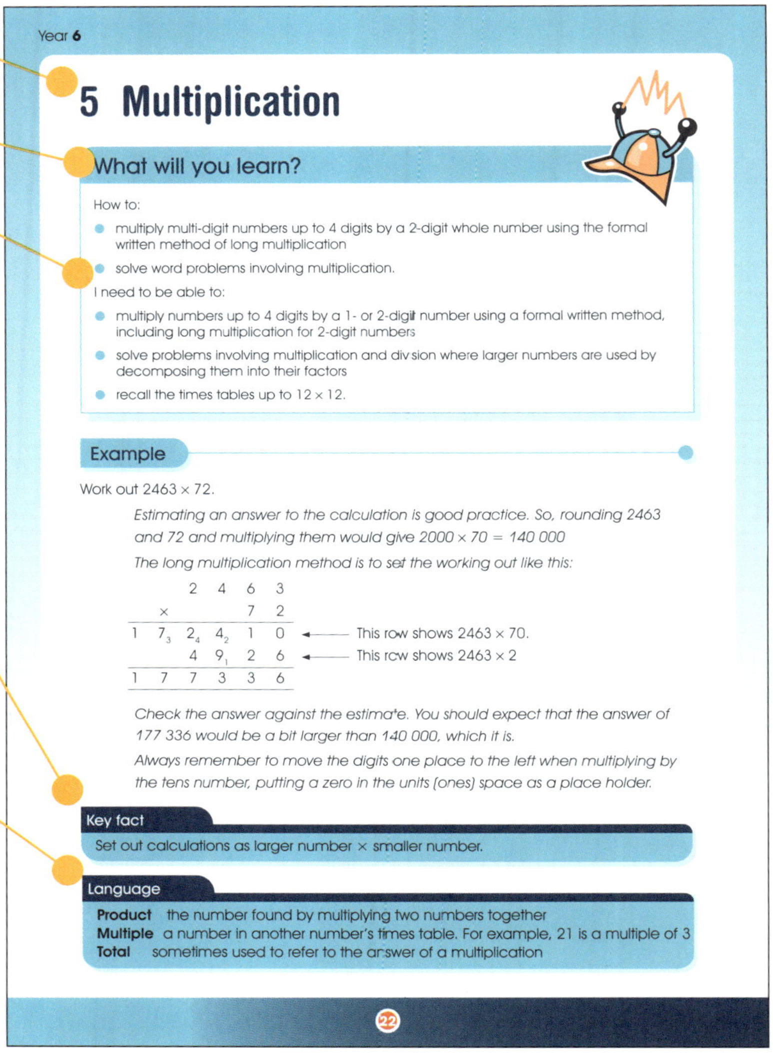
Year 6

5 Multiplication

What will you learn?

How to:

- multiply multi-digit numbers up to 4 digits by a 2-digit whole number using the formal written method of long multiplication
- solve word problems involving multiplication.

I need to be able to:

- multiply numbers up to 4 digits by a 1- or 2-digit number using a formal written method, including long multiplication for 2-digit numbers
- solve problems involving multiplication and division where larger numbers are used by decomposing them into their factors
- recall the times tables up to 12 × 12.

Example

Work out 2463 × 72.

Estimating an answer to the calculation is good practice. So, rounding 2463 and 72 and multiplying them would give 2000 × 70 = 140 000

The long multiplication method is to set the working out like this:

		2	4	6	3	
	×			7	2	
1	7_3	2_4	4_2	1	0	← This row shows 2463 × 70.
		4	9_1	2	6	← This row shows 2463 × 2
1	7	7	3	3	6	

Check the answer against the estimate. You should expect that the answer of 177 336 would be a bit larger than 140 000, which it is.

Always remember to move the digits one place to the left when multiplying by the tens number, putting a zero in the units (ones) space as a place holder.

Key fact

Set out calculations as larger number × smaller number.

Language

Product the number found by multiplying two numbers together
Multiple a number in another number's times table. For example, 21 is a multiple of 3
Total sometimes used to refer to the answer of a multiplication

22

Follow these simple rules if you are using the book for revising.

1. Read each page carefully. Give yourself time to take in each idea.
2. Learn the key facts and ideas. Ask your teacher or mum, dad or the adult who looks after you if you need help.
3. Concentrate on the things you find more difficult.
4. Only work for about 20 minutes at a time. Take a break and then do more work.

If you get most of the **On track** questions right then you know you are working at the expected level for the year. Well done – that's brilliant! If you get most of the **Aiming high** questions right, you are working at the top of expectations for your year. You're doing really well!

The **Using and applying** questions are often more challenging and ask you to explain your answers or think of different ways of answering. The questions give you the chance to use and apply your learning by answering mathematical problems.

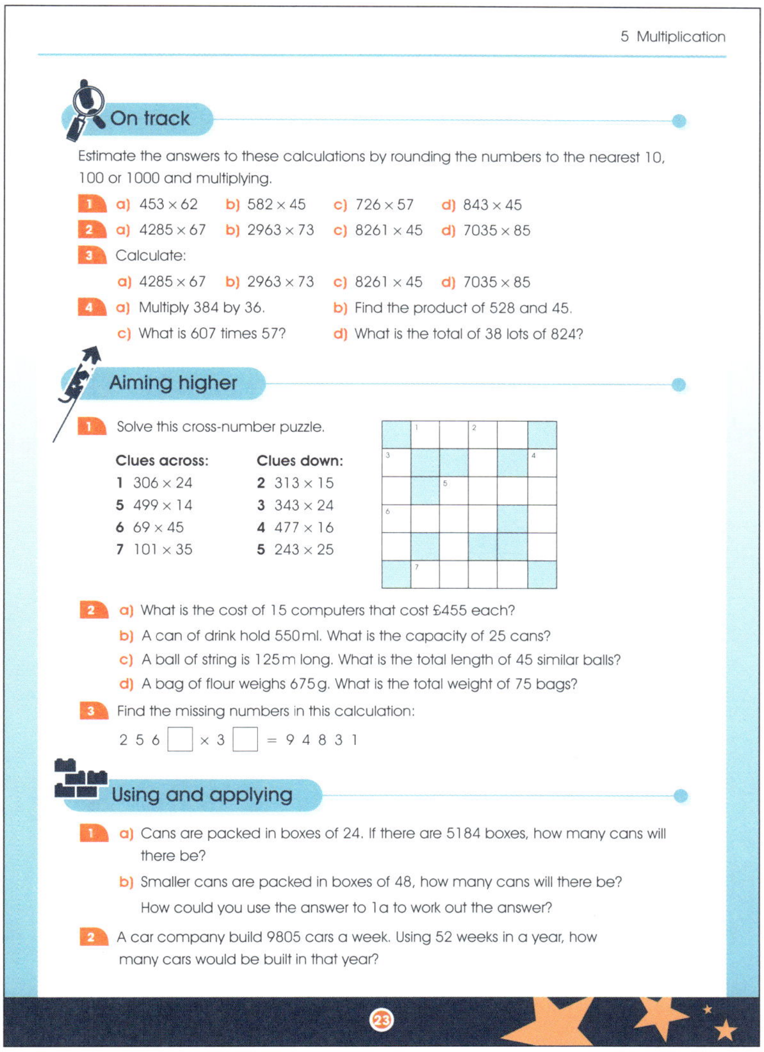

5 Multiplication

On track

Estimate the answers to these calculations by rounding the numbers to the nearest 10, 100 or 1000 and multiplying.

1 a) 453 × 62 b) 582 × 45 c) 726 × 57 d) 843 × 45

2 a) 4285 × 67 b) 2963 × 73 c) 8261 × 45 d) 7035 × 85

3 Calculate:

a) 4285 × 67 b) 2963 × 73 c) 8261 × 45 d) 7035 × 85

4 a) Multiply 384 by 36. b) Find the product of 528 and 45.

c) What is 607 times 57? d) What is the total of 38 lots of 824?

Aiming higher

1 Solve this cross-number puzzle.

Clues across:
1 306 × 24
5 499 × 14
6 69 × 45
7 101 × 35

Clues down:
2 313 × 15
3 343 × 24
4 477 × 16
5 243 × 25

2 a) What is the cost of 15 computers that cost £455 each?

b) A can of drink hold 550 ml. What is the capacity of 25 cans?

c) A ball of string is 125 m long. What is the total length of 45 similar balls?

d) A bag of flour weighs 675 g. What is the total weight of 75 bags?

3 Find the missing numbers in this calculation:

2 5 6 □ × 3 □ = 9 4 8 3 1

Using and applying

1 a) Cans are packed in boxes of 24. If there are 5184 boxes, how many cans will there be?

b) Smaller cans are packed in boxes of 48, how many cans will there be? How could you use the answer to 1a to work out the answer?

2 A car company build 9805 cars a week. Using 52 weeks in a year, how many cars would be built in that year?

23

The answers to all the questions are in the pull-out section in the middle of this book.

Follow these simple rules if you want to know how well you are doing.

1. Work through the questions.
2. Check your answers with your teacher or using the answer booklet in the middle of the book.
3. Keep a record of how well you do.
4. Write down anything you are finding difficult and work through the chapter again to see if you can find the answer. If you are still finding it hard, ask your teacher for help.

1 Place value and numbers

What will you learn?

How to:

- identify the value of each digit to three decimal places and multiply and divide numbers up to three decimal places by 10, 100, 1000 where the answers are up to three decimal places
- multiply one-digit numbers with up to two decimal places by whole numbers
- read, write, order and compare numbers up to 10 million and determine the value of each digit
- identify common factors, common multiples and prime numbers.

I need to be able to:

- find the effect of dividing a one- and two-digit number by 10 and 100
- read, write, order and compare numbers to at least 1,000,000 and determine the value of each digit
- identify multiples and factors, including all factor pairs
- know and use the vocabulary of prime numbers, prime factors and composite (non-prime) numbers
- establish whether a number up to 100 is prime and recall prime numbers up to 19.

Examples

1 What is the value of the 6 in the number 8,765,432?

You may find it useful to use a place value table:

Millions	Hundred thousands	Ten thousands	Thousands	Hundreds	Tens	Units
8	7	6	5	4	3	2

The 6 is in the column of ten thousands so its value is 60 thousands.

Note that large numbers are normally written in groups of three digits with a small space between each group.

2 Calculate 3.72×6

You can calculate this as 372 x 6, but remember 3.72 is a hundred times smaller than 372, so your answer will need to be one hundred times smaller too:

$$\begin{array}{r} 372 \\ \times \quad 6 \\ \hline 2232 \end{array}$$

then

$$2232 \div 100 = 22.32$$

New Curriculum

Primary Mathematics

Learn, practise and revise

Year 6

Trevor Dixon

RISING STARS

Rising Stars UK Ltd, part of Hodder Education, an Hachette UK Company
Carmelite House, 50 Victoria Embankment, London, EC4Y 0DZ

www.risingstars-uk.com

Published 2013
Reprinted 2014, 2015 (twice)

Author: Trevor Dixon
Maths consultant: Sarah-Anne Fernandes, Routes to Success, Sutton
Text design: Green Desert Ltd
Cover design: West 8 Design
Illustrations: Oxford Design and Illustrators
Publisher: Camilla Erskine

British Library Cataloguing in Publication Data.
A CIP record for this book is available from the British Library.

ISBN: 978-0-85769-677-9

Printed by Craft Print Pte Ltd, Singapore

3 Find a common multiple of 4 and 10.

The first multiples of 4 are:

4 8 12 16 20 24 28 32 36 40 44

The first multiples of 10 are:

10 20 30 40 50 60 70 80 90 100 110

20 and 40 are common to both lists of multiples, so they are common multiples.

4 Find a common factor of 24 and 30

The factors of 24 are:	*1*	*2*	*3*	*4*	*6*	*8*	*12*	*24*
The factors of 30 are:	*1*	*2*	*3*	*5*	*6*	*10*	*15*	*30*

1, 2, 3 and 6 are common to both lists, so they are common factors.

5 List the prime numbers less than 10

2, 3, 5 and 7 are the prime numbers less than 10 – they all have only two factors.

The other numbers less than 10 have more or less than two factors.

Key facts

Multiplying by 10 moves digits one column to the left;
multiplying by 100 moves digits two columns to the left;
multiplying by 1000 moves digits three columns to the left…

Dividing by 10 moves digits one column to the right;
dividing by 100 moves digits two columns to the right;
dividing by 1000 moves digits three columns right…

Language

Tenths (t) are $\frac{1}{10}$ of a unit
Hundredths (h) are $\frac{1}{100}$ of a unit
Thousandths (th) are $\frac{1}{1000}$ of a unit

Remember: the decimal fraction number names below zero are the same as the names above zero but use lower case letters.

Common factor a factor which is a factor of two numbers, for example 3 is a common factor of 12 and 15
Common multiple a number that is a multiple of at least two numbers, for example a common multiple of 4 and 6 is 12
Prime number has only two factors – itself and 1.
7 is a prime number because the only factors are 1 and 7.
1 is not a prime number – it has only 1 factor – itself

On track

1 Here is a number:

23,849,401

Use the number to complete these calculations and write the answer in digits.

a) Add twenty.
b) Add thirty thousand.
c) Subtract two million.
d) Subtract five hundred thousand.

2 Multiply each of these numbers by

i) 10 ii) 100 iii) 1000

a) 4 b) 0.64 c) 1.3 d) 1.01 e) 10.2 f) 102

3 Divide each of these numbers by:

i) 10 ii) 100 iii) 1000

a) 4 b) 0.64 c) 1.3 d) 1.01 e) 10.2 f) 102

4 Copy and complete these expressions:

a) $93 \times \square = 9300$
b) $\square \times 10 = 74.8$
c) $4800 \div \square = 48$
d) $\square \div 100 = 0.0947$
e) $1.008 \div \square = 0.01008$
f) $\square \div 100 = 0.431$

5 What is the place value of the digit 4 in each of these numbers?

a) 40,000 b) 4.6 c) 8463 d) 8.463 e) 42,135,869

6 Find the answers to:

a) 9.2×4 b) 18.32×6 c) 12.56×4 d) 57.94×8

7 Write these numbers in order of size, smallest first.

1421 512 3146 598 4

8 Find a common multiple of:

a) 4 and 5 b) 3 and 8 c) 4 and 9 d) 6 and 8

9 Find common factors of:

a) 12 and 20 b) 24 and 36 c) 15 and 35 d) 18 and 30

10 Which of these numbers are prime numbers?

1 5 9 11 16 17 20

Aiming higher

1 Use the fact that $12 \times 1.27 = 15.24$ to find the value of:

a) 1.2×1.27 b) 0.12×1.27 c) 1.2×0.127

2 Here is a number:

37,548,392

Use the number to complete these calculations and write the answer in digits.

a) Add twenty. **b)** Add four million.

c) Add four thousand. **d)** Subtract twenty million.

e) Subtract fifty thousand. **f)** Subtract six hundred thousand.

3 Here are 6 digits: 2 5 0 4 6 9

a) Write down the smallest six-digit whole number you can, using each digit once only.

b) Write down the largest six-digit whole number you can, using each digit once only

4 The lowest common multiple is the common multiple that has the lowest value.

Find the lowest common multiple of:

a) 3, 4 and 5 **b)** 3, 5 and 6 **c)** 6, 8 and 9 **d)** 2, 5 and 7

5 Look at the numbers in the circles, identify their factors and find the common factor that will fit in the square.

a)

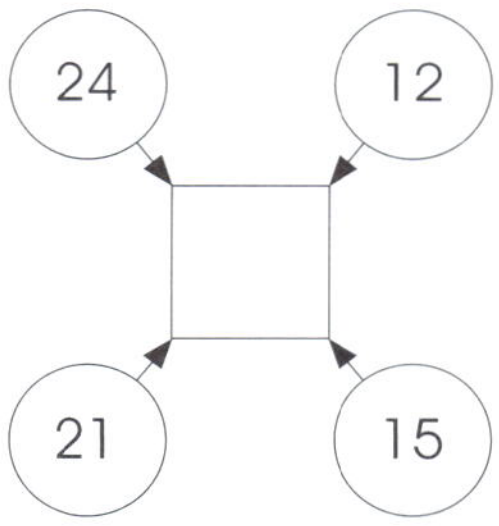

b)

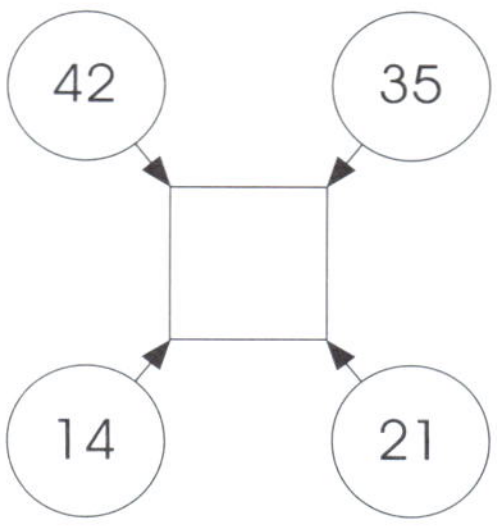

c)

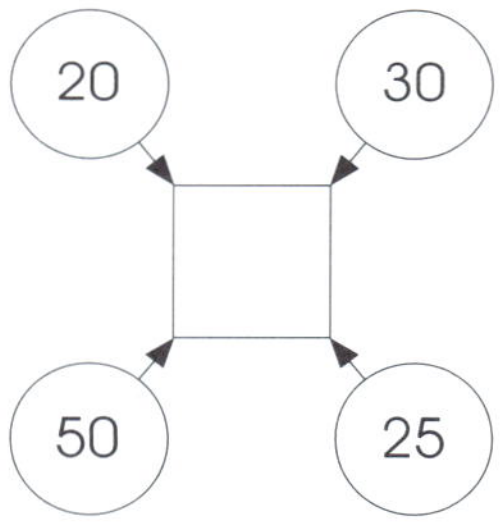

6 Add any two prime numbers less than 10 to make:

a) a multiple of 5 **b)** a multiple of 4 **c)** a multiple of 3.

Using and applying

1 Fatima has to do some work on multiplying and dividing by 10 and 100.

Her brother said:

'To multiply by 10, add a zero, so 6 x 10 = 60.'

'To divide by 10, take the zero off, so 60 ÷ 10 = 6.'

Fatima took his advice and did the following calculations:

a) $2.7 \times 100 = 2.700$ **b)** $3.0 \div 10 = 3$ **c)** $3.05 \div 10 = 3.5$

What answers should she have written down?

2 Fractions

What will you learn?

How to:

- add and subtract fractions with different denominators and mixed numbers, using the concept of equivalent fractions
- multiply simple pairs of proper fractions, writing the answer in its simplest form
- divide proper fractions by whole numbers
- associate a fraction with division to calculate decimal fraction equivalents for a simple fraction.

I need to be able to:

- recognise mixed numbers and improper fractions and convert from one form to the other
- compare and order fractions whose denominators are all multiples of the same number
- add and subtract fractions with the same denominator and related fractions
- multiply proper fractions with the same denominator and related fractions
- read and write decimal numbers as fractions.

Examples

1 a) Work out $\frac{3}{8} + \frac{1}{4}$

First find the common denominator – a number that both 4 and 8 are factors of or divide into.

The first number for this is 8. $\frac{3}{8}$ has a denominator of 8 so we need to change $\frac{1}{4}$ to eighths.

You can do this by setting it out like this:

$\frac{1}{4} = \frac{}{8}$ *The denominator 4 has become a denominator of 8.*

It has been multiplied by 2.

So, we need to multiply the numerator by 2, this gives

$\frac{1}{4} = \frac{2}{8}$

So $\frac{3}{8} + \frac{1}{4} = \frac{3}{8} + \frac{2}{8} = \frac{5}{8}$

b) Work out $5\frac{1}{3} - 1\frac{3}{4}$

You can complete this using this strategy:

$$5\frac{1}{3} - 1\frac{3}{4} = 4\frac{1}{3} - \frac{3}{4}$$ *First, subtract the whole numbers.*

$$= 4\frac{4-9}{12}$$ *Next, find a common denominator and change the $\frac{1}{3}$ to $\frac{3}{4}$.*

$$= 3\not{4}\frac{12+4-9}{12}$$ *Take 1 from 4 and change it into twelfths.*

$$= 3\frac{7}{12}$$ *Complete the calculation with the numerators.*

2 Work out $\frac{1}{4} \times \frac{2}{5}$

$$\frac{1}{4} \times \frac{2}{5} = \frac{2}{20}$$ *First, multiply the two numerators and then multiply the two denominators.*

$$= \frac{1}{10}$$ *Then, you can simplify the fraction, dividing by the common factor of 2 to get a final answer.*

3 Work out $\frac{1}{3} \div 5$

$$\frac{1}{3} \div 5 = \frac{1}{3} \div \frac{5}{1}$$ *Change the 5 units into a fraction.*

$$= \frac{1}{3} \times \frac{1}{5}$$ *The simplest strategy is to invert the dividing fraction and change the division to a multiplication.*

$$= \frac{1}{15}$$ *Complete the calculation as in example 2.*

4 Simplify $\frac{20}{25}$

Simplifying a fraction means re-writing the fraction using numbers of a smaller value, though you need to remember you are not making the fraction smaller, but finding an equivalent fraction. So, find a common factor of 20 and 25 – this is 5. Dividing 20 and 25 by 5 means $\frac{4}{5}$ is the simplified fraction.

5 Change $\frac{5}{8}$ so the denominator is 40.

Find an equivalent fraction for $\frac{5}{8}$ with a denominator of 40.

$8 \times 5 = 40$, so we need to multiply the numerator by 5 too.

$$\frac{5 \times 5}{8 \times 5} = \frac{25}{40}$$

6 Change $\frac{7}{8}$ into a decimal.

A fraction can sometimes be seen as another way of writing a division.

So $\frac{7}{8}$ is another way of asking 'What is 7 divided by 8?'

Set it out as a division calculation and then find the answer:

$$\begin{array}{r} 0.875 \\ 8\overline{)7.{}^{7}0{}^{6}0{}^{4}0} \end{array}$$

So $\frac{7}{8}$ is 0.875

Key facts

Equivalent fractions have the same value.

To compare fractions, use equivalent fractions with a common denominator or convert them into decimals.

A fraction is in its lowest terms when there is no equivalent fraction with a smaller denominator.

Language

Numerator the top number of a fraction

Denominator the bottom number of a fraction

Equivalent the same value as

Simplify means to write a fraction in its '**lowest terms**' when the numerator and denominator have no more common factors, such as $\frac{6}{12}$ is equivalent to $\frac{3}{6}$, $\frac{2}{4}$, $\frac{1}{2}$ ..., but simplifying $\frac{6}{12}$, or writing it in its lowest terms, gives the answer $\frac{1}{2}$.

Factor a number that divides exactly into another

Cancel divide both numbers in a fraction by the same factor

On track

1 Work out:

a) $1\frac{1}{4} + 2\frac{1}{2}$ b) $2\frac{3}{5} + 4\frac{1}{2}$ c) $3\frac{3}{4} - 1\frac{1}{3}$

2 Work out:

a) $\frac{1}{4} \times \frac{3}{7}$ b) $\frac{4}{7} \times \frac{2}{5}$ c) $\frac{5}{6} \times \frac{1}{4}$

3 Simplify these fractions:

a) $\frac{4}{12}$ b) $\frac{5}{15}$ c) $\frac{4}{20}$ d) $\frac{6}{24}$

e) $\frac{10}{25}$ f) $\frac{8}{20}$ g) $\frac{9}{24}$ h) $\frac{18}{24}$

4 Change these fractions so they all have a denominator of 20.

a) $\frac{1}{4}$ b) $\frac{2}{5}$ c) $\frac{3}{4}$ d) $\frac{7}{10}$

5 Change these fractions so they all have a denominator of 100.

a) $\frac{1}{4}$ b) $\frac{1}{5}$ c) $\frac{3}{4}$ d) $\frac{17}{20}$

Aiming higher

1 Work these out. Give your answers as proper fractions or mixed numbers in their lowest terms.

a) $\frac{2}{3} \times \frac{5}{7}$ b) $\frac{1}{8} \times \frac{5}{6}$ c) $\frac{5}{8} \div \frac{3}{4}$ d) $\frac{7}{15} \div \frac{2}{3}$

2 Josh has some number cards.

1	2	3	4	5	6

He uses the cards to make fractions that are equivalent to $\frac{1}{3}$.

What could the equivalent fractions have been? Find five.

You can use a number card more than once and have numerators and denominators of one or two digits.

3 Here are some fractions:

$\frac{15}{40}$ $\frac{8}{32}$ $\frac{12}{32}$ $\frac{12}{40}$ $\frac{9}{30}$ $\frac{8}{20}$ $\frac{6}{24}$ $\frac{12}{30}$ $\frac{9}{24}$ $\frac{16}{40}$

Place the fractions in the table so all the equivalent fractions are in the correct column.

Equivalent fractions of $\frac{3}{10}$	Equivalent fractions of $\frac{2}{5}$	Equivalent fractions of $\frac{1}{4}$	Equivalent fractions of $\frac{3}{8}$

4 Change these fractions to their decimal equivalents.

a) $\frac{3}{5}$ **b)** $\frac{3}{4}$ **c)** $\frac{5}{8}$ **d)** $\frac{4}{5}$

5 Order these fractions, starting with the smallest:

a) $\frac{1}{2}$ $\frac{3}{4}$ $\frac{5}{6}$ $\frac{2}{3}$ **b)** $\frac{3}{4}$ $\frac{4}{5}$ $\frac{7}{10}$ $\frac{13}{20}$

Using and applying

1 Joanna has some sweets.

$\frac{1}{4}$ of her sweets are red, $\frac{2}{5}$ are orange and the rest are yellow.

What fraction of her sweets are yellow?

2 Work out:

a) the area of this rectangle

b) the perimeter of this rectangle.

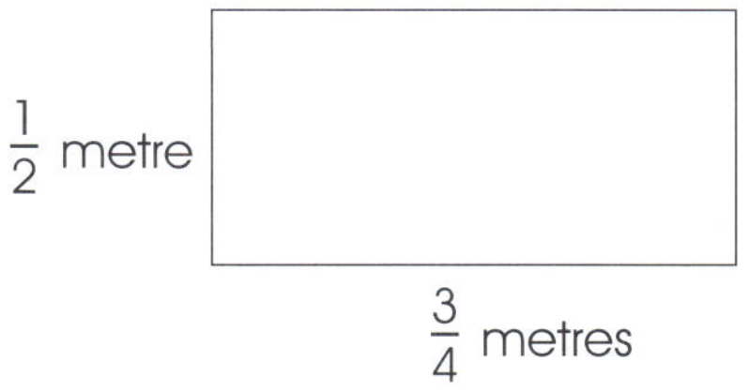

3 Copy and complete:

a) $\frac{2}{5} = \frac{}{20} = \frac{20}{}$ **b)** $\frac{3}{8} = \frac{}{24} = \frac{24}{}$ **c)** $\frac{5}{6} = \frac{}{30} = \frac{30}{}$

4 **a)** $\frac{1}{8}$ of a number is 25. What is the number?

b) $\frac{3}{8}$ of a number is 18. What is the number?

3 Percentages, and Finding fractions and percentages

What will you learn?

How to:

- recall and use equivalences between simple fractions, decimals and percentages, including different contexts
- solve problems involving a calculation of percentages of whole numbers or measures such as 15% of 360 and the use of percentages for comparison.

I need to be able to:

- recognise the per cent symbol (%) and understand that per cent relates to 'number of parts per hundred', and write percentages as a fraction with denominator hundred and as a decimal fraction
- solve problems which require knowing percentage and decimal equivalents of $\frac{1}{2}$, $\frac{1}{4}$, $\frac{1}{5}$, $\frac{2}{5}$, $\frac{3}{5}$, $\frac{4}{5}$ and those with a denominator of a multiple of 10 or 25.

Examples

1 What is £30 as a percentage of £120?

Think 'This is £30 out of £120' and it is easier to see this can be written as a fraction.

$\frac{30}{120} = \frac{1}{4}$ *By using the common factor of 30, you can simplify the fraction to* $\frac{1}{4}$

Next, we can change the fraction into a decimal by dividing 1 by 4.

$$\begin{array}{r} 0.\,2\,5 \\ 4\overline{)1.^{1}0^{2}0} \end{array}$$

So $\frac{1}{4}$ *is the same as 0.25*

0.25 is the same as $\frac{25}{100}$, *which is the same as 25%*

Remember, there are other ways to do this:

- *You could divide 30 by 120, if you were using a calculator.*
  This would give you 0.25.
- *You could multiply the decimal by 100 to change it into a percentage.*

2 30% of cheddar cheese is fat.

Calculate the amount of fat in 250 g of cheddar cheese.

30% is 3 × 10% and 10% $= \frac{1}{10}$

$\frac{1}{10}$ *of 250 = 25, so 3 ×* $\frac{1}{10}$ *of 250 = 75 g*

or

30% $= \frac{30}{100} = 0.3$

So 30% of 250 g = 0.3 × 250 g = 75 g

3 Find $\frac{2}{3}$ of 24.

You might like to think of this as a picture.

This block shows the whole amount – for this question that is 24.

First, we need to split the whole number into thirds.

This is the same as dividing the number 24 by 3.

$24 \div 3 = 8$

So, each third is 8.

8	8	8

$8 \times 3 = 24$

The question asks for $\frac{2}{3}$ *of 24.*

8	8	8

$8 \times 2 = 16$

$\frac{2}{3}$ *of 24 is 16.*

The quick way to find a fraction of a number is to:

- *divide by the denominator*
- *multiply by the numerator.*

Key facts

A percentage is a fraction with a denominator of 100.
Change fractions into percentages by multiplying by 100.
Change percentages into fractions by dividing by 100.
Change fractions into decimals by dividing the numerator by the denominator.

E.g. $\frac{3}{4}$ as a percentage is $\frac{3}{4} \times 100\% = 75\%$.

$\frac{3}{4}$ as a decimal is $3 \div 4 = 0.75$.

Language

Percentage per hundred or out of a hundred

Numerator the top number of a fraction

Denominator the bottom number of a fraction

Equivalent the same value as

On track

1 Which two fractions are equivalent to 0.7?

$\frac{7}{10}$ $\frac{1}{70}$ $\frac{70}{100}$ $\frac{1}{7}$

2 Write these as percentages.

a) 5 kg out of 200 kg b) 3 cm out of 12 cm

3 Amy gets 48 marks out of 60 in a test. Tom gets 56 marks out of 70 in a different test.

Who scored the highest percentage? Show your working

4 a) What percentage of £10 is £2?

b) What percentage of £2 is £10?

5 Write down the fraction in this list with a value greater than 75%.

$\frac{3}{4}$ $\frac{7}{10}$ $\frac{8}{100}$ $\frac{70}{100}$ $\frac{8}{10}$ $\frac{55}{100}$

6 20% of beef is fat. Calculate the amount of fat in 850 g of beef.

7 Copy and complete these sentences.

a) 20% of 80 is ____. b) 20% of ____ is 80.

8 Find:

a) $\frac{3}{4}$ of £48 b) 40% of £750 c) 25% of 44 m

9 Flowers in a garden display are arranged in the following proportions:

red 10% yellow 35% pink 20% purple 25% white 10%

There are 200 flowers altogether.

Find how many there are of each colour.

Aiming higher

1 Copy and complete this table to show equivalent fractions, decimals and percentages.

Fraction	Decimal	Percentage
Three eighths		
	0.45	
		40%
One fifth		

2 What percentages are the following?

a) 2p of £1 **b)** 1 cm of 1 m **c)** 15 mm of 1 cm

d) 50p of £5 **e)** 100 m of 1 km **f)** 20 g of 1 kg

3 Children in Year 6 could choose to go to a theme park or the seaside for an end-of-term trip. The table shows what happened.

	Theme park	Seaside
Girls	24	36
Boys	36	29

a) What was the total number of pupils who chose a theme park?

b) What percentage of these were girls?

c) What was the total number of girls in Year 6?

d) What percentage of the girls chose the seaside?

e) What was the total percentage of pupils who chose a theme park?

Show your working.

4 Copy and complete these statements.

a) 20 is 10% of ____. **b)** 12 is 60% of ____.

c) 4 is 25% of ____. **d)** 120 is 80% of ____.

Using and applying

1 Here are some symbols.

×	O	O	×	O	×	×	×	×	O	×	×	O
	×	O	O	×	O	×	×	×	×	O	×	×

Calculate the **a)** fraction **b)** decimal **c)** percentage of the symbols that are ×.

2 This is how Beth works out 15% of 360.

10% of 360 is 36.

5% of 360 is 18.

So 15% of 360 is 36 + 18 = 54.

Use Beth's method to work out 17.5% of 720.

3 Max buys a flute that costs £400.

a) First he pays a deposit of 30%. How much is this?

b) Then he makes 12 monthly payments of £30.
How much do these payments come to?

c) What is the total of the deposit and the monthly payments?

d) How much extra does he pay for the flute?

4 Proportion and ratio

What will you learn?

How to:

- solve problems involving the relative size of two quantities, including similar shapes.
- solve problems involving unequal sharing and grouping.

I need to be able to:

- recognise equivalent ratios and reduce a ratio to its lowest terms
- recognise and use division in the context of fractions, percentages and ratio.

Examples

1 Three pens cost 84 pence. How much do five pens cost?

Here are two possible ways of solving this problem.

- *Find what one pen costs:* *1 pen costs 84p ÷ 3 = 28p.*

  Then find what five pens cost: *5 pens cost 28p × 5 = £1.40*

- *Write down this fraction:* $\frac{\text{new number}}{\text{old number}}$

  Multiply the cost by the fraction: 84p × $\frac{5}{3}$ *= £1.40*

  The new number is larger than the old number, so you are ***scaling up***.

2 Tom and Dev share £20, so that Dev gets three times as much as Tom. How much do they each get?

In this question, the ratio needed is 1:3.

You might like to think of each part of the ratio as shares that Tom and Dev are going to get.

So, in total there are four shares. (1 + 3 = 4)

£20 divided into four shares means each share is worth £5. (20 ÷ 4 = 5)

Tom has one share, which is £5. (5 x 1 = 5) Dev has three shares which is £15. (5 x 3 = 15)

As a check, you can add the shares together; you should get the total you started with. (5 + 15 = 20)

Key facts

The simplest way to solve ratio and proportion problems is to find the value, or cost, of one thing and then multiply by the new number of things.
Doubling and halving are also useful techniques. For example: if 200 g of sherbert lemons cost £1.80, how much do 150 g cost?

Halve to find cost of 100 g:	90p
Halve again to find cost of 50 g:	45p
Add to find cost of 150 g:	£1.35

Language

Ratio compares a part to a part

Proportion compares a part to the whole. For example:
in a class of 30 children, there are 20 boys and 10 girls.
The **ratio** of boys to girls is 20 to 10 or 2 to 1, which is often written as 2:1.
The **proportion** of boys in the class is 20 out of 30 or 2 out of 3, which is usually written as $\frac{2}{3}$.

Lowest terms this means that the fraction or ratio should be simplified by dividing both parts by the largest number that divides into both – the highest common factor.

On track

1 Amy is making strawberry ice cream for ten people.

Strawberry ice cream for six people

600 g strawberries	200 ml cream
240 g sugar	100 ml water

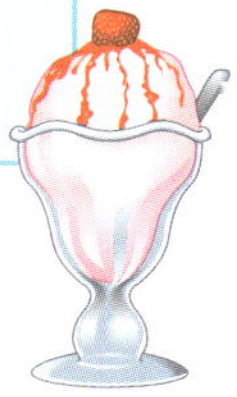

a) What weight of strawberries will she need?

b) How much sugar will she need?

2 Four cookies cost £2.40.

How much would you pay for:

a) 8 cookies b) 20 cookies c) 2 cookies d) 10 cookies

3 In a zoo there are 30 monkeys and some gorillas and chimpanzees.

The ratio of monkeys to gorillas is 6 to 1.

The ratio of monkeys to chimpanzees is 5 to 2.

a) How many gorillas are there? b) How many chimpanzees are there?

Twelve monkeys are moved to another zoo.

What are the new ratios of:

c) monkeys to gorillas? d) monkeys to chimpanzees?

4 A drink is made by adding water and orange juice in the ratio of 5:1.

How much drink will there be if:

a) 200 ml of juice is used
b) 2.5 litres of water is used
c) 0.15 litre of water is used
d) $\frac{1}{2}$ litre of juice is used?
e) If 1800 ml of drink is made, how much juice will be used?
f) If 2.4 litres of drink is made, how much water will be used?

5 An oblong is 5 cm long and 3 cm wide. The dimensions are kept in proportion.

What will the new length and width be if the shape is drawn:

a) 3 times larger
b) 6 times larger
c) 12 times larger

Aiming higher

1 For every four cans of drink that are bought, a sticker is given away.

a) How many cans would have to be bought to collect 12 stickers?
b) If 20 cans of drink were bought, how many stickers are collected?

2 This a recipe to make cheese scones.

Re-write this recipe to make:

a) 40 scones
b) 15 scones
c) 25 scones

Cheese scones
(Makes 10 scones)

- 200 g flour
- 30 g cheese
- 50 g butter
- 150 ml milk

3 Amy is making a necklace from black and white beads.

She makes groups of three black beads and two white beads.

Each group is followed by a silver disc. The picture shows part of the necklace.

Amy has 45 black beads to use. Work out how many of the others she needs.

a) white beads
b) silver discs

4 Copy and complete these statements:

a) 1:3 is equivalent to 5:?
b) 2:5 is equivalent to 6:?
c) 4:5 is equivalent to ?:20
d) 9:36 is equivalent to 1:?

5 A 5 cm square is enlarged. By what scale factor (how many times bigger has it got?) if it is

a) 20 cm square
b) 7.5 cm square
c) 22.5 cm square

Using and applying

1 Zaphyr bought 50 m of climbing rope for £80.

a) How much would 150 m of climbing rope cost?

b) How much rope could he get for £100?

Show how you worked your answers out.

2 A window cleaner charges £3.60 for cleaning 4 windows.

a) What will he charge for cleaning 10 windows?

b) If the window cleaner earned £18 an hour, how many windows does he clean in an hour?

3 Check the pattern in this statement:

3 is to 8, as 9 is to 24

Complete these statements:

a) 5 is to 6, as 15 is to ___.

b) ___ is to 12, as 2 is to 6

c) 8 is to 9, as 32 is to ___.

d) 5 is to ___, as 1 is to 12

What could the missing numbers in this statement be?

e) 4 is to ___, as 6 is to ___.

4 Here is a way to make purple paint.

Mix red paint and blue in the ratio 4 to 1.

a) How much red paint do you mix with 50 ml of blue paint?

b) How much blue paint do you mix with 1200 ml of red paint?

Show how you worked your answers out.

5 A prize is divided between Tom and Amy so that Tom gets three times as much as Amy.

a) Write down the ratio of the small share (Amy's) to the large share (Tom's).

b) The prize was £24. Can you work out how much Amy and Tom would each get?

6 **a)** Rob, Amir and Josef share £80 in the ratio of 5:3:2.

How much do they each get?

b) Sally, Uma and Jo share some money.

Sally gets £40, Uma gets £16 and Jo gets £8.

Which ratio did they use to divide the money?

Write the ratio in its simplest terms.

7 The sides of an oblong are in the ratio of 4:3. The oblong has a length of 12 cm and is increased by a scale factor of 2.5. What will the increased width be?

5 Multiplication

What will you learn?

How to:

- multiply multi-digit numbers up to 4 digits by a 2-digit whole number using the formal written method of long multiplication
- solve word problems involving multiplication.

I need to be able to:

- multiply numbers up to 4 digits by a 1- or 2-digit number using a formal written method, including long multiplication for 2-digit numbers
- solve problems involving multiplication and division where larger numbers are used by decomposing them into their factors
- recall the times tables up to 12 × 12.

Example

Work out 2463 × 72.

Estimating an answer to the calculation is good practice. So, rounding 2463 and 72 and multiplying them would give 2000 × 70 = 140 000

The long multiplication method is to set the working out like this:

		2	4	6	3	
	×			7	2	
1	7_3	2_4	4_2	1	0	← This row shows 2463 × 70.
		4	9_1	2	6	← This row shows 2463 × 2
1	7	7	3	3	6	

Check the answer against the estimate. You should expect that the answer of 177 336 would be a bit larger than 140 000, which it is.

Always remember to move the digits one place to the left when multiplying by the tens number, putting a zero in the units (ones) space as a place holder.

Key fact

Set out calculations as larger number × smaller number.

Language

Product the number found by multiplying two numbers together
Multiple a number in another number's times table. For example, 21 is a multiple of 3
Total sometimes used to refer to the answer of a multiplication

On track

Estimate the answers to these calculations by rounding the numbers to the nearest 10, 100 or 1000 and multiplying.

1 a) 453 × 62 b) 582 × 45 c) 726 × 57 d) 843 × 45

2 a) 4285 × 67 b) 2963 × 73 c) 8261 × 45 d) 7035 × 85

3 Calculate:

a) 4285 × 67 b) 2963 × 73 c) 8261 × 45 d) 7035 × 85

4 a) Multiply 384 by 36. b) Find the product of 528 and 45.

c) What is 607 times 57? d) What is the total of 38 lots of 824?

Aiming higher

1 Solve this cross-number puzzle.

Clues across:

1 306 × 24

5 499 × 14

6 69 × 45

7 101 × 35

Clues down:

2 313 × 15

3 343 × 24

4 477 × 16

5 243 × 25

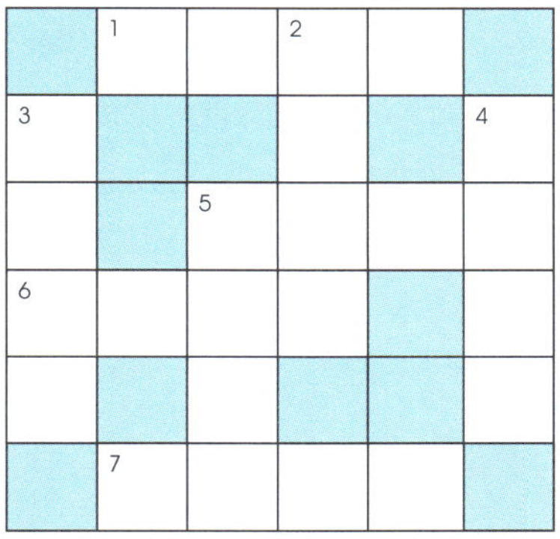

2 a) What is the cost of 15 computers that cost £455 each?

b) A can of drink hold 550 ml. What is the capacity of 25 cans?

c) A ball of string is 125 m long. What is the total length of 45 similar balls?

d) A bag of flour weighs 675 g. What is the total weight of 75 bags?

3 Find the missing numbers in this calculation:

2 5 6 ☐ × 3 ☐ = 9 4 8 3 1

Using and applying

1 a) Cans are packed in boxes of 24. If there are 5184 boxes, how many cans will there be?

b) Smaller cans are packed in boxes of 48, how many cans will there be?

How could you use the answer to 1a to work out the answer?

2 A car company build 9805 cars a week. Using 52 weeks in a year, how many cars would be built in that year?

6 Division

What will you learn?

How to:

- divide numbers up to 4 digits by a 2-digit whole number using long division and interpret remainders as whole number remainders, fractions, decimals or by rounding as appropriate for the context
- use written division methods in cases where the answer has up to two decimal places
- round any number to a required degree of accuracy
- use estimation to check answers to calculations and determine, in the context of a problem, whether an answer should be rounded or written as a fraction or a decimal.

I need to be able to:

- divide numbers up to 4 digits by a one-digit number using short division and interpret remainders appropriately for the context
- round any number up to 1 000 000 to the nearest 10, 100, 1000, 10 000 and 100 000
- use rounding to check answers to calculations and determine, in the context of the problem, levels of accuracy.

Examples

1 Work out 87.23 ÷ 27

You can complete calculations using the strategy of long division.

```
       3 . 2 3
    ___________
2 7 | 8 7 . 2 1
      8 1
      ---
        6   2
        5   4
        -----
            8 1
            8 1
            ---
              0
```

a. *Start by dividing 87 by 27.* *(27 x 3 = 81)*
Record 81 below 87 and record 3 in units column of the answer.

b. *Subtract 87 – 81.* *87 – 81 = 6.*
The '6' needs to be with the 2 to make 62, but we lack space so bring the 2 to the 6.

c. *Put the decimal point in the answer.*

d. *Ignore the decimal point in 6.2 and divide 62 by 27*
(27 x 2 = 54)
Record 54 below 62 and record 2 in the tenths column of the answer.

e. *Subtract 62 – 54.* *62 – 54 = 8.*
The '8' needs to be with the 1 to make 81, but we lack space so bring the 1 to the 8.

f. *Divide 81 by 27.* *(27 x 3 = 81)*
Record 81 below 81 and record 3 in hundredths column of the answer.
Subtract 81 – 81 = 0.

2 Work out 247 ÷ 17.

```
     1 4
1 7 |2 4 7
   1 7
     7 7
     6 8
       9
```

a. *Start by dividing 24 by 17.* *(17 × 1 = 17)*
Record 17 below 24 and record 1 in tens column of the answer.

b. *Subtract 24 – 17.* *24 – 17 = 7.*
The '7' needs to be with the 7 in the units column to make 77, but we lack space so bring the 7 to the 7.

c. *Divide 77 by 17* *(17 x 4 = 68)*
Record 68 below 77 and record 4 in the units column of the answer.

d. *Subtract 77 – 68.*
77 – 68 = 9.

There is a remainder of 9.

What you do with the remainder will depend on the context of the problem.

3 Look at these problems:

a) *247 sweets are shared among 17 friends, how many do they get each?*

Answer: 14 remainder 9

You can't divide sweets up so these are left over.

b) *247 mini-pizzas are divided among 17 tables. How many pizzas will be on each table?*

Answer: $14\frac{9}{17}$

You can divide pizzas up. Dividing by 17 makes seventeenths and there are 9 pieces left over.

c) *£247 is divided among 17 friends. How much do they get each?*

Answer: £14.53

Money always needs to be written with two decimal places. The third decimal place is 9, so round up to 14.53.

d) *Divide 247 by 17. Give your answer to one decimal place.*

Answer: 14.5

Here the second decimal place is 2, so round down to 14.5.

Key facts

Remember to line up the decimal points when you divide decimals.
Remember to think about the context of a problem when deciding how to write the answer.

Language

Integers whole numbers

On track

1 Find the answers to these calculations.

a) £1275 ÷ 25 b) 3672 kg ÷ 18 c) £2124 ÷ 36

d) Oranges cost 35p each. How many oranges can be bought for £21.00?

2 Answer these calculations, giving your answer as a decimal.

a) £1595 ÷ 44 b) 2418 kg ÷ 52 c) 3225 ml ÷ 60

d) 1177 m of rope is cut into 55 equal lengths. How long is each length?

3 Answer these calculations, giving each answer as a fraction.

a) 472 ÷ 5 b) 8342 ÷ 7 c) 835 ÷ 9 d) 7403 ÷ 6

e) 3348 kilograms of potatoes are put into 25 sacks. How many kilograms are in each sack?

4 Work out the answers to the following calculations. Give your answers to two decimal places.

a) 1460 ÷ 18 b) 5339 ÷ 26 c) 6322 ÷ 71 d) 5278 ÷ 60

Aiming higher

1 Look at this number chain.

7110 —÷45— 158 —÷ 25— 6.32

Copy and complete these chains.

a) 9252 —÷ 18— ___ —÷ 40— ___

b) 3556 —÷ 14— ___ —÷ 50— ___

c) ___ —÷ 27— ___ —÷ 40— 18.5

2 A dance raised £9765 by selling tickets at £35. How many people went to the dance?

3 2280 fans want to travel to watch their football team by coach.
The coaches have 48 seats.
How many coaches will need to be booked?

4 It is usually said that there are 52 weeks in a year of 365 days.
Is this actually so? How many weeks are there exactly in 365 days? Give your answer using a fraction.

Using and applying

1 Find the answer to these calculations.

$5204 \div 16$ $2712 \div 48$ $1274 \div 35$ $1441 \div 44$

a) Give the answer as a fraction.

b) Give the answer as a decimal.

c) What does this tell you about the fraction and the decimal?

2 $3048 \div 48 = 63.5$

Use this fact to give nearest multiple of 48 below 3048.

3 a) $4680 \div 40$

$40 = 10 \times 2 \times 2$

so, dividing by 10 and then dividing by 2 twice will give the same result.

Try it and see.

b) Give a way of dividing by 24, by dividing by smaller numbers.

c) Give a way of dividing by 36, by dividing by smaller numbers.

d) Give a way of dividing by 18, by dividing by smaller numbers.

e) Give a larger number that is the same as dividing by 7, then 3, then 2

7 Harder calculations

What will you learn?

How to:

- use knowledge of the order of operations to carry out calculations involving the four operations
- solve word problems involving addition, subtraction, multiplication and division.

I need to be able to:

- solve problems involving addition, subtraction, multiplication and division and a combination of these, including understanding the meaning of the equals sign.

Examples

1 We often carry out calculations that involve more than one operation.

For example: $25 + 45 \times 275$

You need to know whether to add 25 and 45 and multiply the answer by 275, or to multiply 45 by 275 and then add on 25.

Calculations are always completed in a certain order. This way you will know which calculation comes first.

Use this order of operations:

Brackets **I**ndices **D**ivision **M**ultiplication **A**ddition **S**ubtraction

Remember this by using the word **BIDMAS**.

So, $25 + 45 \times 275$ means you must complete the multiplication first.

$$25 + 45 \times 275 = 25 + 12\,375$$
$$= 12\,400$$

2 $(25 + 45) \times 275$ means you must complete the addition first, because it's in brackets.

$$(25 + 45) \times 275 = 70 \times 275$$
$$= 19\,250$$

3 4^2 means 4×4, or we sometimes say 'four squared'.

The small ^{2} tells you how many times 4 is multiplied by itself.

$$4^2 = 4 \times 4 = 16$$

A small ^{3} means a number is multiplied by itself three times. This is called 'cubed', so 6^3 is 6 cubed.

$$6^3 = 6 \times 6 \times 6 = 216$$

4 Tom buys a magazine for £3.95 and a pen for £1.29.
How much change will he get from £10?

This is a two-step problem. First, you need to add the costs of £3.95 and £1.29 together and then subtract the total from £10.

If this is recorded as a calculation, brackets are needed to show the first step:

$$10 - (3.95 + 1.29)$$

Key fact

BIDMAS is an abbreviation standing for Brackets, Indices, Division, Multiplication, Addition and Subtraction. It tells you the order of operations in a calculation.

Language

Index (plural – indices) small numbers written above and to the right of other numbers. They tell you how many times to multiply the number by itself.
$5^2 = 5 \times 5 = 25$ and $5^3 = 5 \times 5 \times 5 = 125$

On track

1 Use the correct order of operations to calculate the following.

a) $4 + 6 \times 8 - 10 \div 2$ b) $(26 + 34) \div (76 - 36)$ c) $(45 - 26) \times (58 - 23)$
d) $4256 - 34 \times 23$ e) $(2586 - 66) \div (409 - 381)$ f) $803 - 8128 \div 32$
g) $(3119 - 569) \div 75$ h) $(65 + 78) \times (372 - 286)$ i) $(325 + 543) \times 43$

2 For each of these problems:

i) set out the problem using brackets and numbers only
ii) solve the problem.

a) Dev has 6 sets of cards. In each set there are 25 colour cards and 45 black and white cards. How many cards does he have altogether?

b) Mary bakes 240 small buns for a summer fair. 35 of the buns are burned, so she throws them away. She packs the rest into bags of 4 buns. How many bags will she be able to sell at the fair?

c) On a Monday, each train leaving Kings Cross for Newcastle has 9 coaches. 3 of the coaches are first class and the rest are second class. There are 17 trains between 04:00 and 12:00 and 20 trains from 12:00 until 23:00. How many second-class coaches travel to London from Newcastle each day?

d) At a school, a class of children have a tea party. There are 150 sandwiches. In the class there are 16 girls and 14 boys. If the sandwiches are shared equally among the children, how many will they get each?

Aiming higher

1 Use the correct order of operations to calculate the following.
Where there are two sets of brackets, you will need to complete the inside set of brackets ( ) first, before you complete the square outside brackets [ ].

a) $[5 \times (5 + 7) + 15] \times 5 + 30$
b) $35 \times [50 - 4 \times (15 - 10)]$
c) $100 - [80 \div (10 \times 10 - 80)]$
d) $300 - [15 \times 80 \div (16 + 4) - 10]$

2 Find the answers to these calculations.

a) $5^2 + 6^2$ b) $8^2 - 4^2$ c) $7 + 4^2$ d) $(7 + 4)^3$
e) $(20 - 8)^2$ f) $10^2 - (8 - 5)^2$ g) $7^2 - (5 - 3)^2$ h) $8^3 - 8$

3 Find the answers to these calculations.

a) $\frac{5 \times (6 + 14)}{50}$ b) $\frac{(30 - 3) \div 9}{3}$ c) $\frac{(30 \div 6) + (49 \div 7)}{(50 \div 25)}$

d) $\frac{45 \div (15 - 6)}{(35 \div 7)}$ e) $\frac{(17 + 8) \times (34 - 9)}{(2.5 \times 2)}$ f) $\frac{100 \times (45 - 20)}{125 + 375}$

4 For each of these problems:

i) set out the problem using brackets and numbers only
ii) solve the problem.

a) In a school there are 185 boys and 163 girls that have school dinner. They each pay £10.50 for their dinners each week. How much money is this altogether?
b) An airline has a fleet of three types of aircraft. There are 12 that have 853 seats, 24 that have 313 and 32 that have 150. How many seats is this in total?
c) Ewan has £885. He bought a computer for £350 and a printer for £95. He put a quarter of what he had left into the bank. How much did he put in the bank?
d) Rav borrows some money to pay for a car that costs £12 650 and a holiday that costs £1750. He is going to repay the money over 36 months. How much will he have to repay each month if he pays no interest on the loan?

Using and applying

1 See how many different answers you can find by adding brackets to the following.

a) 10 + 5 × 10 ÷ 5 + 10 – 5

b) 25 – 5 + 10 ÷ 5 × 20 – 10

c) 24 + 8 ÷ 2 – 6 + 4 × 10

2 Use the numbers to make each of the number sentences correct.

a) Use 3, 5 and 8 in (___ + ___) × ___ = 39

b) Use 4, 8 and 24 in (___ – ___) ÷ ___ = 4

c) Use 4, 8, 10 and 16 in (___ – ___) × (___ – ___) = 24

d) Use 3, 5, 6 and 8 in (___ + ___ – ___) × ___ = 55

3 a) Here are seven cards.

(   )   ×   +   10   15   20

Use your knowledge of the order of operations to arrange the cards to give the largest possible total.

b) Here are seven cards.

(   )   –   ÷   10   20   40

Use your knowledge of the order of operations to arrange the cards to give the smallest possible positive answer.

8 Negative numbers

What will you learn?

How to

- use negative numbers in context and calculate intervals across zero
- solve number problems and practical problems in context.

I need to be able to:

- interpret negative numbers in context, count forwards and backwards with positive and negative whole numbers through zero
- solve number problems and practical problems in context, counting forwards and backwards with positive and negative whole numbers through zero.

Example

Here are some city temperatures for the same time on one day in December.

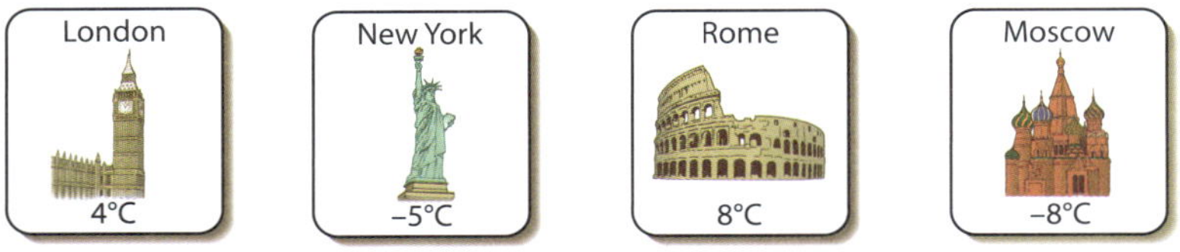

Which was the coldest city? Which was the warmest city? How can you tell?

What was the difference in temperature between them?

The coldest city was Moscow; the warmest city was Rome.

You could draw a number (temperature) line and mark on each temperature.

The difference between them is 16 °C.

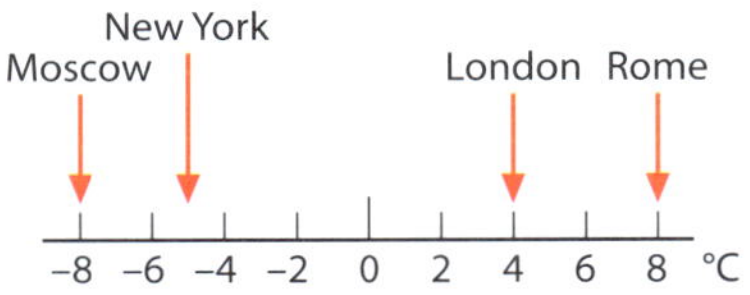

Key facts

Negative numbers are shown to the left of zero on a horizontal number line or below zero on a vertical number line.

If you count along a number line from left to right, the numbers get bigger; if you count back from right to left, the numbers get smaller.

Language

Positive numbers numbers greater than zero
Negative numbers numbers less than zero
Integers whole numbers

On track

1 Here is a number line. Only the 0 is shown.

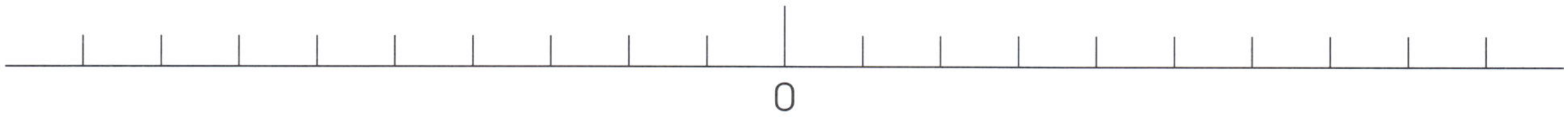

Copy this number line and add these numbers to it.

a) 7 **b)** –5 **c)** 4 **d)** –3 **e)** –8 **f)** 2

2 What temperature is:

a) 6 °C below 3 °C ? **b)** 12 °C below 7 °C? **c)** 18 °C below 3 °C?

d) 13 °C above –4 °C? **e)** 15 °C above –12 °C? **f)** 25 °C above –17 °C?

3 Temperatures are taken on one day in each of five cities.

City	Temperature at midnight	Temperature at midday
Birmingham	–2 °C	7 °C
Leeds	–7 °C	5 °C
Newcastle	–9 °C	5 °C
Norwich	–1 °C	10 °C
Nottingham	–4 °C	9 °C

a) Which city had the greatest temperature rise between midnight and mid-day?

b) Which city had the smallest temperature rise from midnight to mid-day?

4 Find the missing numbers

a) 7 – ☐ = –12 **b)** ☐ – 15 = –9 **c)** 12 – ☐ = –20

d) ☐ – 26 = –8 **e)** (40 – 65) + ☐ = –5

5 What is the difference between:

a) 10 and –5? **b)** 6 and –6? **c)** 0 and –20

d) –7 and –16 **e)** –4 and –40

Aiming higher

1 You may need a calculator for this question.

In a magic square the numbers in each column, each row and each diagonal all add up to the same number, called the magic number.

In this magic square there are both positive and negative numbers. The magic number is –6.

There are some numbers missing in this magic square. Each column, row and diagonal adds up to –6. Copy and complete it.

0		
–7	–2	
		–4

2 There is a lift in an office block. The ground floor is numbered 0, the first floor is 1, the second floor is 2 and so on. There are three basement floors used as a car park. The first floor down is numbered –1.

a) How many floors is it from the basement floor –2 to floor 6?

b) How many floors is it from floor 10 to basement floor –1?

c) The lift starts at basement floor –3 and goes up 9 floors. Which floor does it stop at?

d) The lift starts at basement floor –1 and moves 2 floors. Which two floors might it have arrived at?

3 League positions for football teams are normally decided by the number of points they have. If two teams are level on points, their position is decided by goal difference. Goal difference is the difference between the number of goals scored (goals for) and the numbers of goals let in (goals against).

Work out the goal difference for teams in this league.

		Played	Goals For	Goals Against	Points	Goal Difference
a)	**Rovers**	18	61	23	45	
b)	**Rangers**	18	58	24	41	
c)	**United**	18	45	18	36	
d)	**City**	18	44	28	36	
e)	**Town**	18	35	35	31	
f)	**Wanderers**	18	27	28	26	
g)	**West End**	18	26	35	25	
h)	**Albion**	18	15	43	16	
i)	**Athletic**	18	12	51	12	
j)	**County**	18	9	63	9	

4 The balance column on a bank statement tells you how much money you have. Sometimes you have taken out more than you have in your account. This is recorded by showing a negative balance.

Complete the balance column for this bank statement.

	Date	Paid in	Paid out	Balance
a)	1st Sept			£54.40
b)	2nd Sept		£25.00	
c)	8th Sept		£40.00	
d)	12th Sept	£75.00		
e)	17th Sept		£125.00	
f)	18th Sept		£5.50	
g)	25th Sept		£35.00	
h)	30th Sept	£975.00		

Using and applying

1 Complete these number sequences with the next **two** values.

a)	35	20	5	–10	☐	☐
b)	5	3.5	2	0.5	☐	☐
c)	95	65	35	5	☐	☐
d)	27	19	11	3	☐	☐

2 A sequence **starts at 30.**

The rule is: **keep subtracting 8.**

Write the first two numbers in the sequence that are **less than zero**.

How did you find them?

30
22
14
......

3 A sequence follows this rule: 'Halve the number and subtract 2'.

a) Complete the sequence following this rule.

4 0 ☐ ☐ ☐

b) What do you notice about the size of the intervals between the numbers?

4 **a)** The difference between –6 and another number is 7. What could the two numbers be?

b) The difference between –15 and another number is 8. What could the two numbers be?

c) The difference between 18 and another number is 25. What could the two numbers be?

9 Algebra

What will you learn?

How to:

- express missing number problems algebraically
- find pairs of numbers that satisfy number sentences involving two unknowns
- use simple formulae expressed in words
- generate and describe linear number sequences.

I need to be able to:

- solve problems involving addition, subtraction, multiplication and division and a combination of these, including understanding the meaning of the equals sign.

Examples

1 Find the value of a.

$5a + 3 = 18$

Try to solve this problem by re-arranging the numbers so the equation is 'a = ___'.

$5a + 3 = 18$ *First you subtract +3.*

You can do this by subtracting 3, but remember you must subtract 3 from both sides of the equation.

$5a + 3 \mathbf{- 3} = 18 \mathbf{- 3}$

$5a = 15$ *Now divide 5 into 5a, which is 5 × a.*

You will do this by dividing by 5, and again remember to divide both sides of the equation by 5.

$5a \div \mathbf{5} = 15 \div \mathbf{5}$

$a = 3$ *The answer is 3.*

2 Find the value of b, when $c = 3$.

$b = 4c + 6$

In this equation you need to substitute the 'c' for 3.

So, $b = 4 \times 3 + 6$

$b = 18$

3 Describe how these patterns grow.

Each pattern adds 2 more blocks, so it is growing in multiples of 2.

Pattern number (p)	1	2	3
Number of blocks (B)	3	5	7

The number of blocks (B) for any pattern number (p) is equal to twice the pattern number plus one.

As a formula, this would be:

$B = 2p + 1$

4 Which two numbers when multiplied together equal 12, but add up to 7?

The pairs of numbers multiply to give 12 are:

1×12 $\quad 2 \times 6$ $\quad 3 \times 4$

Only one of these pairs total 7:

3 and 4

Key fact

Letters stand for numbers that we don't know yet. They are called unknowns.
$4y$ is the same as '4 multiplied by y'.

Language

Equation a mathematical sentence that uses symbols (=) to say two things are of the same value. E.g. $5 \times 3 = 20 - 5$

Formula numbers and symbols used as instructions to solve a calculation. E.g. $P = 2(l + w)$ is a formula to find the perimeter, P, of a rectangle using the length, l, and width, w. 2 is a constant because you always double the length and the breadth to find the perimeter, but l and b are variables, because they change for each rectangle.

Substitute replacing letters in formulae and equations with numbers. E.g. Solve $x = 3 + b$, when $b = 8$. Replacing b with 8 means $x = 3 + 8 = 11$

On track

1 a) Max is thinking of a number.

He adds 15 to the number and multiplies the total by 20. He gets 400. What is the number Max is thinking of?

b) Omar is thinking of a number.

He multiplies the number by 6 and then divides the answer by 5. He gets 12. What is the number Omar is thinking of?

2 Solve the following:

a) $5a = 60$ b) $12b = 72$ c) $8c = 40$ d) $7d = 140$

3 Follow these instructions to solve problems.

A gardener charges £25 for each visit and £15 an hour for every hour she works.

How much does she charge if she works for:

i) 4 hours **ii)** 8 hours **iii)** 1 hour?

4 **a)** Solve $4r + 7$ when $r = 9$ **b)** Solve $15s - 20$ when $s = 5$

c) Solve $8t + 12 - 9$ when $t = 11$ **d)** Solve $12u - 30$ when $u = 7$

5 The shapes below stand for numbers.

Calculate the value of the shapes.

a) □ × △ = 20 □ + △ = 12, so □ = ___ and △ = ___

b) ⬡ × ⏢ = 32 ⬡ + ⏢ = 18, so ⬡ = ___ and ⏢ = ___

c) ◇ ÷ ○ = 4 ◇ − ○ = 9, so ◇ = ___ and ○ = ___

d) ◺ × □ = 60 ◺ − □ = 11, so ◺ = ___ and □ = ___

Aiming higher

1 Solve the following:

a) $6a + 45 = 105$ **b)** $12b - 35 = 85$ **c)** $30c - 70 = 80$

d) $2d - 200 = 100$ **e)** $10e - 140 = 10$ **f)** $100f - 500 = 500$

g) $4g + 2.5 = 10.5$ **h)** $6h - 5.5 = 6.5$

2 A, B, C and D are all different whole numbers.

$A+B = 10$ $B+C=5$ $C+D= 8$ $D+A= 13$

Find the values of A, B, C, and D.

3 Cakes are sold in a shop for double the cost of the ingredients and then £3 is added.

The shopkeeper uses this formula: $P = 2c + 3$

P is the price and c is the cost of the ingredients.

Find the price of a cake if the ingredients cost:

a) £2 **b)** £3.50 **c)** £5.25 **d)** £4.75

A different cake shop uses this formula: $P = 3c + 2$

Find the price of the cakes in the second shop if the ingredients cost:

e) £2 **f)** £5.50 **g)** £3.40 **h)** £6.25

4 Find the value of each symbol.

◎ ◎ ◎ ◎ ◎ = 600 ◎ = ___

◎ ✪ ✪ ✪ ✪ = 360 ✪ = ___

Using and applying

1 The grid shows a pattern that grows.

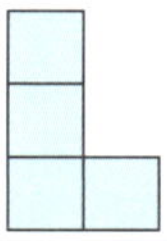	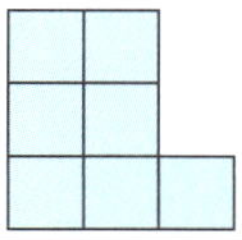	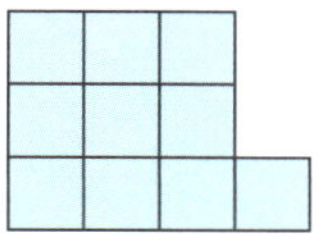	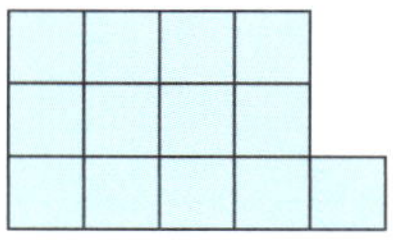
Pattern number 1	**Pattern number 2**	**Pattern number 3**	**Pattern number 4**
Number of squares 4	Number of squares ___	Number of squares ___	Number of squares ___

a) Complete the number of squares needed for Pattern numbers 2, 3 and 4.

b) How many squares would be needed for Pattern number 5?

c) Write a rule to show how you could find out how many squares would be in any pattern number.

d) Change your rule into a formula beginning with $S =$, where S is the number of squares. Use p for the pattern number.

e) Use your formula to find how many squares will be in the Pattern number 35.

Use the facts and complete the equation:

2

• $x = 2y$ • $3y = z$ • $x = 12$ $z =$ ___	• $p = 5r$ • $2r = s$ • $s = 20$ $p =$ ___	• $a = 2b$ • $4b = c$ • $a = 8$ $c =$ ___	• $4d = e$ • $3e = f$ • $f = 24$ $d =$ ___

3 Bill has three packages.

Package C is twice the weight of Package B.

Package B is three times the weight of Package A.

Package B weighs 6 kg.

What is the total weight of the three packages?

10 Angles

What will you learn?

How to:

- find unknown angles involving angles in any triangles, in quadrilaterals and regular polygons
- find unknown angles where they meet at a point, are on a straight line and are vertically opposite.

I need to be able to:

- know angles are measured in degrees; estimate and measure them and draw a given angle, writing its size in degrees (°)
- identify:
  - multiples of 90°
  - angles at a point on a straight line and $\frac{1}{2}$ a turn (total 180°)
  - angles at a point and one whole turn (total 360°)
  - reflex angles
  - compare different angles.

Examples

1 Two of the angles in a triangle are 35° and 45°.

What is the size of the third angle?

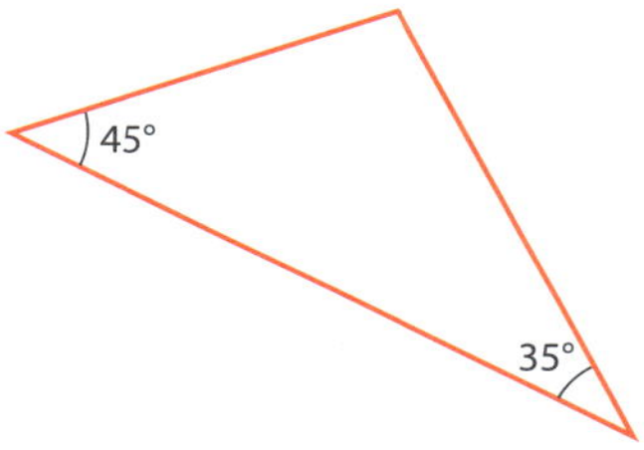

Angles in a triangle add up to 180°.

35° + 45° = 80°

So the third angle = 180° − 80° = 100°

2 There are nine equal angles around a point.

What is the size of each angle?

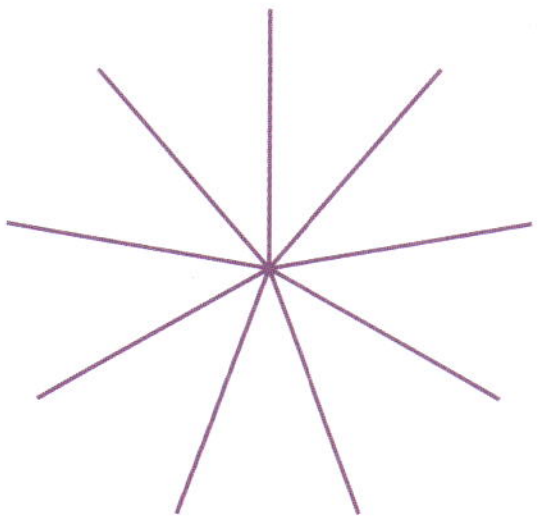

Angles around a point add up to 360°.

The nine angles are equal.

So each angle is 360° ÷ 9 = 40°.

3 Three angles in a quadrilateral have been identified.
What is the size of the fourth angle?

Angles of a quadrilateral add up to 360°.

70° + 90° + 90° = 250°

So the fourth angle = 360° – 250° = 110°

Mathematics Study guide: Year 6

Answer Booklet

1 Place value and numbers

On track

1 **a)** 23 849 421 **b)** 23 879 401
c) 21 849 401 **d)** 23 349 401

2 **a)** i) 40 ii) 400 iii) 4000
b) i) 6.4 ii) 64 iii) 640
c) i) 13 ii) 130 iii) 1300
d) i) 10.1 ii) 101 iii) 1010
e) i) 102 ii) 1020 iii) 10 200
f) i) 1020 ii) 10 200 iii) 102 000

3 **a)** i) 0.4 ii) 0.04 iii) 0.004
b) **i)** 0.064 ii) 0.0064 iii) 0.00064
c) **i)** 0.13 ii) 0.013 iii) 0.0013
d) **i)** 0.101 ii) 0.0101 iii) 0.00101
e) **i)** 1.02 ii) 0.102 iii) 0.0102
f) **i)** 10.2 ii) 1.02 iii) 0.102

4 Student's answers checked as in 1 and 2
a) 100 **b)** 7.48 **c)** 100
d) 9.47 **e)** 100 **f)** 43.1

5 **a)** 40 000 or 4 tens of thousands or forty thousand
b) 4 or 4 units
c) 400 or 4 hundred
d) $\frac{4}{10}$ or 4 tenths
e) 40 000 000 or 40 million

6 **a)** 36.8 **b)** 109.92
c) 50.24 **d)** 463.52

7 4, 512, 598, 1421, 3146

8 **a)** 20 (and all multiples of 20)
b) 24 (and all multiples of 24)
c) 36 (and all multiples of 36)
d) 24 (and all multiples of 24)

9 **a)** 2 and 4 **b)** 2, 3, 4, 6 and 12
c) 5 **d)** 2, 3 and 6

10 5, 11, 17

Aiming higher

1 **a)** 1.524 **b)** 0.1524
c) 0.1524

2 **a)** 37 548 412 **b)** 41 548 392
c) 37 552 392 **d)** 17 548 392
e) 37 498 392 **f)** 36 948 392

3 **a)** 204, 569 **b)** 965, 420

4 **a)** 60 **b)** 30
c) 72 **d)** 70

5 **a)** 3 **b)** 7 **c)** 5

6 **a)** 2 + 3 = 5
b) 5 + 7 = 12 or 3 + 5 = 8
c) 2 + 7 = 9

Using and applying

1 **a)** 270 – move the digits two places to the left to multiply by 100
b) 0.3 – move the digits one place to the right to divide by 10
c) 0.305 – move the digits one place to the right to divide by 10 and do not remove any zeros acting as place holders

2 Fractions

On track

1 **a)** $3\frac{3}{4}$ **b)** $7\frac{1}{10}$ **c)** $2\frac{5}{12}$

2 **a)** $\frac{3}{28}$ **b)** $\frac{8}{35}$ **c)** $\frac{5}{24}$

3 **a)** $\frac{1}{3}$ **b)** $\frac{1}{3}$ **c)** $\frac{1}{5}$ **d)** $\frac{1}{4}$
e) $\frac{2}{5}$ **f)** $\frac{2}{5}$ **g)** $\frac{3}{8}$ **h)** $\frac{3}{4}$

4 **a)** $\frac{5}{20}$ **b)** $\frac{8}{20}$ **c)** $\frac{15}{20}$ **d)** $\frac{14}{20}$

5 **a)** $\frac{25}{100}$ **b)** $\frac{20}{100}$ **c)** $\frac{75}{100}$ **d)** $\frac{85}{100}$

Aiming higher

1 **a)** $\frac{10}{21}$ **b)** $\frac{5}{48}$
c) $\frac{20}{24} = \frac{5}{6}$ **d)** $\frac{21}{30} = \frac{7}{10}$

2 The fraction could have been:
$\frac{2}{6}$ $\frac{4}{12}$ $\frac{5}{15}$ $\frac{11}{33}$ $\frac{12}{36}$ $\frac{14}{42}$ $\frac{15}{45}$ $\frac{21}{63}$ $\frac{22}{66}$

3

Equivalent fractions of $\frac{3}{10}$	Equivalent fractions of $\frac{2}{5}$	Equivalent fractions of $\frac{1}{4}$	Equivalent fractions of $\frac{3}{8}$
$\frac{9}{30}$ $\frac{12}{40}$	$\frac{8}{20}$ $\frac{12}{30}$ $\frac{16}{40}$	$\frac{6}{24}$ $\frac{8}{32}$	$\frac{9}{24}$ $\frac{12}{32}$ $\frac{15}{40}$

4 **a)** 0.6 **b)** 0.75
c) 0.625 **d)** 0.8

5 **a)** $\frac{1}{2}$ $\frac{2}{3}$ $\frac{3}{4}$ $\frac{5}{6}$ **b)** $\frac{13}{20}$ $\frac{7}{10}$ $\frac{3}{4}$ $\frac{4}{5}$

Using and applying

1 $\frac{7}{20}$

2 **a)** $\frac{3}{8}m^2$ **b)** $2\frac{1}{2}m$

3 **a)** $\frac{2}{5} = \frac{8}{20} = \frac{20}{50}$
b) $\frac{3}{8} = \frac{9}{24} = \frac{24}{64}$
c) $\frac{5}{6} = \frac{25}{30} = \frac{30}{36}$

4 **a)** 200 **b)** 48

3 Percentages, and Finding fractions and percentages

On track

1 $\frac{7}{10}$ and $\frac{70}{100}$

2 **a)** 2.5% **b)** 25%

3 $\frac{48}{60} = 48 \div 60 = \frac{4}{5} = 0.8 = 80\%$
$\frac{56}{70} = 56 \div 70 = 0.8 = 80\%$
Amy and Tom both scored the same.

4 **a)** 20% **b)** 500%

5 $\frac{8}{10}$

6 170 g

7 **a)** 16 **b)** 400

8 **a)** £36 **b)** £300 **c)** 11 m

9

Red	20
Yellow	70
Pink	40
Purple	50
White	20

Aiming higher

1

Fraction	Decimal	Percentage
Three eighths	0.375	37.5%
$\frac{9}{20}$ or $\frac{45}{100}$	0.45	45%
$\frac{2}{5}$ or $\frac{40}{100}$	0.4 or 0.40	40%
One fifth	0.2 or 0.20	20%

2 **a)** 2% **b)** 1% **c)** 150%
d) 10% **e)** 10% **f)** 2%

3 **a)** 60 **b)** 40% **c)** 60
d) 60% **e)** 48%

4 **a)** 200 **b)** 16 **c)** 20 **d)** 150

Using and applying

1 **a)** $\frac{16}{25}$ **b)** 0.64 **c)** 64%

2 10% of 720 = 72
5% of 720 = 36
2.5% of 720 = 18
72 + 36 + 18 = 126
So, 17.5% of 720 = 126

3 **a)** £120 **b)** £360 **c)** £480 **d)** £80

4 Proportion and ratio

On track

1 **a)** 1000 g or 1 kg **b)** 400 g or 0.4 kg

2 **a)** £4.80 **b)** £12 **c)** £1.20 **d)** £6

3 **a)** 5 gorillas
b) 12 chimpanzees
c) 18 : 5
d) 18 : 12 (simplified to 3 : 2)

4 **a)** 1.2 l (1200 ml) **b)** 3 l (3000 ml)
c) 0.18 l (180 ml) **d)** 3 l (3000 ml)
e) 300 ml (0.3 l) **f)** 2 l (2000 ml)

5 **a)** 15 cm long; 9 cm wide
b) 30 cm long; 18 cm wide
c) 60 cm long; 36 cm wide

Aiming higher

1 **a)** 48 cans **b)** 5 stickers

2

a)	b)	c)
800 g flour	300 g flour	500 g flour
200 g butter	75 g butter	125 g butter
120 g cheese	45 g cheese	75 g cheese
600 g milk	225 g milk	375 g milk

3 **a)** 30 **b)** 15

4 **a)** 15 **b)** 15 **c)** 16 **d)** 4

5 **a)** 4 × scale factor
b) 1.5 × scale factor
c) 4.5 × scale factor

Using and applying

1 **a)** £240 (50 m costs £80. 150 m = 50 m × 3; £80 × 3 = £240)
b) 62.5 m (£80 gets 50 m. £100 ÷ £80 = 1.25, so 50 m × 1.25 = 62.5)

2 **a)** £9 (10 windows ÷ 4 windows = 2.5, so £3.60 × 2.5 = £9)
b) 20 windows (£3.60 ÷ 4 = £0.90 = 90p, so £18 = 1800p, 1800 ÷ 90 = 20)

3 **a)** 18 **b)** 4 **c)** 36 **d)** 60
e) There is an infinite number of answers, but the numbers 4 and 6 must be either:
• multiplied by same number, e.g.

4 × 3 and 6 × 3, so the statement is 4 is to 12, as 6 is to 18 e.g. 4 × 4.5 and 6 × 4.5, so the statement is 4 is to 18, as 6 is to 27
- divided by the same number, e.g. 4 ÷ 2 and 6 ÷ 2, so the statement is 4 is to 2, as 6 is to 3

4 a) 50 ml × 4 = 200 ml
b) 1200 ml ÷ 4 = 300 ml

5 a) 1 : 3
b) Amy received £6 and Tom received £18.

6 a) Tom gets £40, Amir gets £24 and Josef gets £16.
b) 5 : 2 : 1. Find the highest common factor for 40, 16 and 8, which is 8 and divide each of the amounts by 8

7 If the oblong has a length of 12 cm, then the width is 9 cm, using the fact that the ratio of the sides is 4 : 3. Therefore if the sides are scaled up by 2.5, the increased width is 9 cm multiplied by 2.5 = 22.5 cm.

5 Multiplication

On track

1 a) 30 000 b) 30 000
c) 42 000 d) 40 000

2 a) 280 000 b) 210 000
c) 400 000 d) 630 000

3 a) 287 095 b) 216 299
c) 371 745 d) 597 975

4 a) 13 824 b) 23 760
c) 34 599 d) 31 312

Aiming higher

1

■	[1] 7	3	[2] 4	4	■
[3] 8	■	■	6	■	[4] 7
2	■	[5] 6	9	8	6
[6] 3	1	0	5	■	3
2	■	7	■	■	2
■	[7] 3	5	3	5	■

2 a) £6825
b) 13 750 ml (13.75 l)
c) 5625 m (5.625 km)
d) 50 625 g (50.625 kg)

3 2563 × 37 = 94 831

Using and applying

1 a) 124 416 cans
b) 248 832
48 is double 24, so double 124 416 to find the answer of 248 832.

2 a) 509 860

6 Division

On track

1 a) £51 (or 5100p)
b) 204 kg
c) £59.00 (or 5900 p)
d) 59 oranges

2 a) £36.25 b) 46.5 kg
c) 53.75 ml d) 21.4 m

3 a) $94\frac{2}{5}$ b) $1191\frac{5}{7}$
c) $92\frac{7}{9}$ d) $1233\frac{5}{6}$
e) $133\frac{23}{25}$ kg

4 a) 81.11 b) 205.35
c) 89.04 d) 87.97

Aiming higher

1 a)
9252 —÷ 18→ **514** —÷ 40→ **12.85**

b)
3556 —÷ 14→ **254** —÷ 50→ **5.08**

c)
19980 —÷ 27→ **740** —÷ 40→ 18.5

2 **279** people

3 **48** coaches. Final coach is half full.

4 **$52\frac{1}{7}$**

Using and applying

1 i) a) $325\frac{1}{4}$ b) 325.25 c) $\frac{1}{4}$ = 0.25
ii) a) $56\frac{1}{2}$ b) 56.5 c) $\frac{1}{2}$ = 0.5
iii) a) $36\frac{2}{5}$ b) 36.4 c) $\frac{2}{5}$ = 0.4
iv) a) $32\frac{3}{4}$ b) 32.75 c) $\frac{3}{4}$ = 0.75

2 0.5 = $\frac{1}{2}$, so 3048 ÷ 48 = 63.5 = $63\frac{1}{2}$ = $63\frac{24}{48}$
3048 – 24 = 3024
3024 ÷ 48 = 63
3024 is the largest multiple of 48 below 3048.

3 a) 4680 ÷ 10 = 468
468 ÷ 2 = 234
234 ÷ 2 = 117
4680 ÷ 40 = 117
b) ÷ 24 = ÷ 3 ÷ 2 ÷ 2 ÷ 2
c) ÷ 36 = ÷ 3 ÷ 3 ÷ 2 ÷ 2
d) ÷ 18 = ÷ 3 ÷ 3 ÷ 2
e) ÷ 7 ÷ 3 ÷ 2 = ÷ 42

7 Harder calculations

On track

1 a) 47 b) 1.5 c) 665
d) 3474 e) 90 f) 549
g) 34 h) 12 298 i) 37 324

2 a) i) 6 x (25 + 45) ii) 420
b) i) (240 – 35) ÷ 4 ii) 51
c) i) (9 – 3) × (17 + 20) ii) 222
d) i) 150 ÷ (16 + 14) ii) 5

Aiming higher

1 a) 405 b) 1050 c) 96 d) 250

2 a) 61 b) 48 c) 23 d) 1331
e) 144 f) 91 g) 45 h) 504

3 a) 2 b) 1 c) 6 d) 1
e) 125 f) 5

4 a) i) (185 + 163) × 10.5 ii) £3654
b) i) (853 × 12) + (313 x 24) + (150 × 32)
ii) 22 548 passengers
c) i) $\frac{885 - (350 + 95)}{4}$
or [885 – (350 + 95)] ÷ 4
ii) £110
d) i) $\frac{12650 + 1750}{36}$
or (12 650 + 1750) ÷ 36
ii) £400

Using and applying

1 Among correct solutions are:
a) 10 + 5 × 10 ÷ (5 + 10 – 5) = 6
(10 + 5) × 10 ÷ (5 + 10 – 5) = 15
10 + 5 × 10 ÷ 5 + (10 – 5) = 25
10 + 5 × 10 ÷ 5 + 10 – 5 = 35
(10 + 5) × 10 ÷ 5 + 10 – 5 = 45
(10 + 5) × (10 ÷ 5 + 10 – 5) = 105
b) 25 – (5 + 10 ÷ 5 × 20 – 10) = –10
25 – 5 + 10 ÷ 5 × (20 – 10) = 40
25 – 5 + 10 ÷ 5 × 20 – 10 = 50
(25 – 5 + 10 ÷ 5) × (20 – 10) = 60
(25 – 5 + 10) ÷ 5 × 20 – 10 = 110
c) 24 + 8 ÷ 2 – (6 + 4) × 10 = –84
(24 + 8) ÷ 2 – 6 + 4 × 10 = 50
24 + 8 ÷ 2 – 6 + 4 × 10 = 62
(24 + 8 ÷ 2 – 6 + 4) × 10 = 260

2 a) (5 + 8) × 3 = 39
b) (24 – 8) ÷ 4 = 4
c) (16 – 4) × (10 – 8) = 24
Also (8 – 4) × (16 – 10) = 24
d) (8 + 6 – 3) × 5 = 55

3 a) (10 + 15) × 20 = 500
b) 40 ÷ (10 – 20) = –4
Also (10 ÷ 20) – 40 = –39.5

8 Negative numbers

1

2 a) –3°C b) –5°C c) –15°C
d) 9°C e) 3°C f) 8°C

3 a) Newcastle b) Birmingham

4 a) 19 b) 6 c) 32
d) 18 e) 20

5 a) 15 b) 12 c) 20
d) 9 e) 36

Aiming higher

1

0	**–1**	**–5**
–7	–2	**+3**
+1	**–3**	–4

2 a) 8 floors b) 11 floors
c) Floor 6 d) Floor 1 or Floor –3

3 a) 38 b) 34 c) 27 d) 16
e) 0 f) –1 g) –9 h) –28
i) –39 j) –54

4

	Date	Paid in	Paid out	Balance
a)	1st Sept			£54.40
b)	2nd Sept		£25.00	£29.40
c)	8th Sept		£40.00	–£10.60
d)	12th Sept	£75.00		£64.40
e)	17th Sept		£125.00	–£60.60
f)	18th Sept		£5.50	–£66.10
g)	25th Sept		£35.00	–£101.10
h)	30th Sept	£975.00		£873.90

Using and applying

1 a) 35 20 5 –10 **–25** **–40**
b) 5 3.5 2 0.5 **–1** **–2.5**
c) 95 65 35 5 **–25** **–55**
d) 27 19 11 3 **-5** **–13**

2 –2, –10
e.g. 'By jumping backwards along a number line' or 'by subtracting 8 each time in my head' or 'by going through the eight-times table backwards and taking 2 off each answer'.

3 a) 4 0 **–2** **–3** **–3.5**
b) The sequence is decreasing by numbers that are halving or dividing by 2.

4 a) 1 and –13 b) –7 and –23
c) 43 and –7

9 Algebra

On track

1 a) 5 b) 10

2 a) a = 12 b) b = 6
c) c = 5 d) d = 20

3 a) i) £85 ii) £145 iii) £40
b) e = 24 b) f = 40
d) g = 46 e) h = 94

4 a) 43 b) 55 c) 91 d) 54

5 For a) think of two numbers that multiply to give 20; it could be 20 × 1, 10 × 2 or 5 × 4, then look at these pairs of numbers and see which pair will add to 12. You will need to use a similar strategy with the other three questions.

Using and applying

1 There are two ways to calculate the answer:

i) See how many tiles fit along the length and the width:
$65 \div 6.5 = 10$, $36 \div 4.5 = 8$
and $10 \times 8 = 80$, so 80 tiles

ii) area of the table top $= 65 \times 36 = 2340\,cm^2$
Area of a tile $= 6.5 \times 4.5 = 29.25\ cm^2$
$2340 \div 29.25 = 80$, so 80 tiles

2 Perimeter = 32 cm, one side is 5 cm, so opposite sides added together = $5 + 5 = 10$ cm.
$32 - 10 = 22$ cm for the other two sides,
$22 \div 2 = 11$ cm for one side.
Area $= 11 \times 5 = 55\,cm^2$

3 Side AB = side BC, both are three times the length of AC or $3 \times$ AC, so the perimeter is $3 \times AC + 3 \times AC + AC = 7 \times AC$.
Perimeter = 56 cm
Length of AC $= 56 \div 7 = 8$ cm,
so AB $= 8 \times 3 = 24$ cm

4 Suitable drawings:

a) Parallelogram could have a base and height of:
28 cm × 1 cm, 14 cm × 2 cm,
7 cm × 4 cm These measurements could be reversed

b) Triangle could have a base and height of:
24 cm × 1 cm,12 cm × 2 cm,
8 cm × 3 cm, 6 cm × 4 cm These measurements could be reversed.

c) Square must be: 6 cm × 6 cm

d) Rectangle could be:
9 cm × 1 cm, 8 cm × 2 cm,
7 cm × 3 cm, 6 cm × 4 cm,
5 cm × 5 cm

5 **a)** If rectangles are made from the squares, they could measure
4 cm × 3 cm (perimeter: 14 cm),
6 cm × 2 cm (perimeter: 16 cm) or
12 cm × 1 cm (perimeter: 26 cm)

b) Yes.

18 Volume

On track

1 **a)** $125\ cm^3$ **b)** $512\ cm^3$
c) $1000\,cm^3$ **d)** $8000\,cm^3$
e) $125000\,cm^3$

2 **a)** $112\,000\,cm^3$
b) $98\,000\,cm^3$ – the water will make a cuboid 70 cm × 40 cm × 35 cm

Aiming higher

1 $1\,200\,000\ cm^3$

2 $64\ cm^3$
To have an area of $16\ cm^2$, the square must be 4 cm × 4 cm, so each side must be 4 cm. The volume will be $4 \times 4 \times 4 = 64\ cm^3$.

Using and applying

1 $240\ cm^3$
Area of triangle $= \frac{1}{2} \times 8 \times 6 = 24\ cm^2$, then multiply the area of the end shape (also the cross-section) by the length of the prism, so $24 \times 10 = 240\ cm^3$

2 Possible dimensions:
18 cm × 2 cm × 1 cm
9 cm × 4 cm × 1 cm
9 cm × 2 cm × 2 cm
6 cm × 6 cm × 1 cm
6 cm × 3 cm × 2 cm
4 cm × 3 cm × 3 cm

19 Interpreting data

On track

1 **a)** 20 **b)** 7 **c)** 13

2 **a)** 120 children
b) Netball and Tennis
c) 30 children, the sector for tennis is a quarter, $120 \div 4 = 30$
d) Athletics
e) 5 children +/–2 children. You can make your estimate by comparing the sizes of the sectors and thinking about the total value.

Aiming higher

1 **a)** 86°F +/–5°F **b)** 60°C +/–5°F
c) The actual temperature is 100°C, but allow +/–3°C
d) The actual temperature is 32°F, but allow +/–3°F

2 **a)** Ash Street School
Ash Street has 200 children, a quarter have a dinner ($200 \div 4 = 50$)
Oak Lane has 80 children, a half have dinner ($80 \div 2 = 40$)
b) i) 105 ii) 28

Using and applying

1

Sandwiches	Size of angle	Number
Beef	15°	**5**
Chicken	45°	**15**
Cheese	105°	**35**
Ham	84°	**28**
Prawn	6°	**2**
Tuna	69°	**23**
Salad	36°	**12**

20 Averages – Mean

On track

1 13.7 seconds

2 The three numbers must total 36, so e.g. 6, 10, 20 or 1, 2, 33 or 11, 12, 13

3 The four numbers must total 20, if three of the numbers ($2 + 3 + 8$) total 13, then the fourth number must be ($20 - 13$) 7.

Aiming higher

1 The total of the eight numbers is $16 \times 8 = 128$
The total of the nine numbers is $20 \times 9 = 180$
The ninth number is $180 - 128 = 52$

2 The total of the seven numbers is $122 \times 7 = 854$
$854 - 146 = 708$
The total of the six numbers is 708, so the mean is $708 \div 6 = 118$

3 The mean of A + B is 50, so A + B = 100
A + B + C = 150, so 100 + C = 150,
so C = 50
Hence, A could equal 40 and B equal 60, or any two amounts that total 100, except 50 + 50.

Using and applying

1 The total of the seven numbers is $17 \times 9 = 119$
The total of the five numbers you can see is 79, so the other two numbers must total ($119 - 79$) = 40, e.g. 0 and 40, 39 and 1, and so on.

2 **a)** The total is $15 \times 4 = 60$, so any four numbers that total 60, e.g. 1 + 1 + 1 + 57 or 15 + 13 + 17 + 15

Using and applying

1 a) 4 faces and 4 vertices, a tetrahedron
b) 6 faces and 6 vertices
c) number of faces = number of vertices = number of sides of base + 1

2 a)

	Faces	Edges	Vertices
Triangular prism	5	9	6
Rectangular prism	6	12	8
Pentagonal prism	7	15	10

b) There are two set of patterns, both quite similar:
- number of faces increases by 1
  number of edges increases by 3
  number of vertices increases by 2
- number of faces is number of sides of the cross-section + 2
  number of edges is the number of sides of the cross-section × 3
  number of vertices is the number of sides of the cross-section × 2

c) i) an octagonal prism (8 sides on shape of cross-section) has 10 (8 + 2) faces, 24 (8 × 3) edges and 16 (8 × 2) vertices.
ii) an icosagonal prism (20 sides on shape of cross-section) has 22 (20 + 2) faces, 60 (20 × 3) edges and 40 (20 × 2) vertices.

3 24 of the smaller cuboids will fit in the larger cuboid.

4 a) 4 cm × 2 cm × 1 cm
b) 2 cm × 3 cm × 6 cm
c) 5 cm × 4 cm × 1 cm

14 Nets of solids

On track

1 Suitable drawings
2 a) rectangle
b) triangles, rectangles
c) square, triangles
d) triangles
3 a) cylinder b) cone

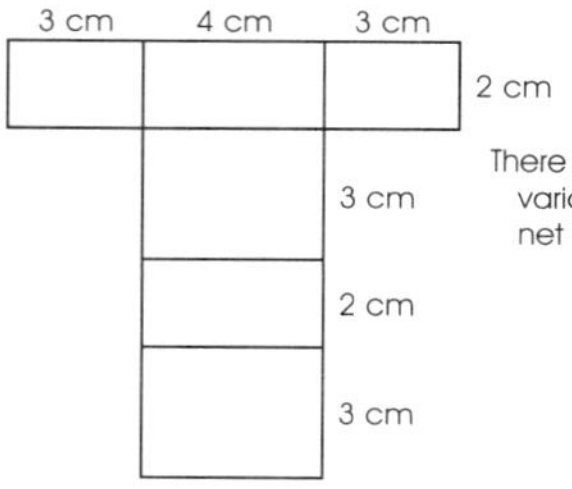

There are 10 other variations for the net of a cuboid.

Aiming higher

1 a) pentagonal-based prism
b) cuboid
c) triangular prism
d) square-based prism
2 B, D
3 A B C D

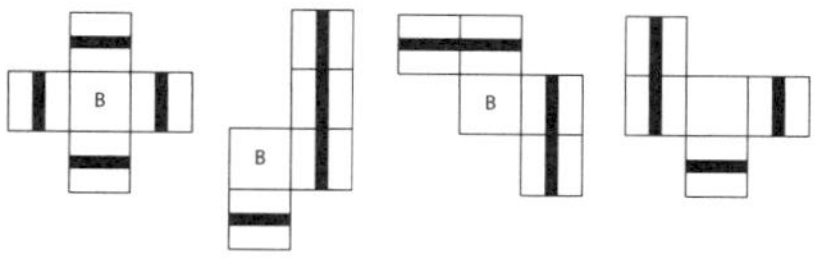

4 a) true b) true c) true d) true

Using and applying

1 A, B, D
2 a) b) c) d)

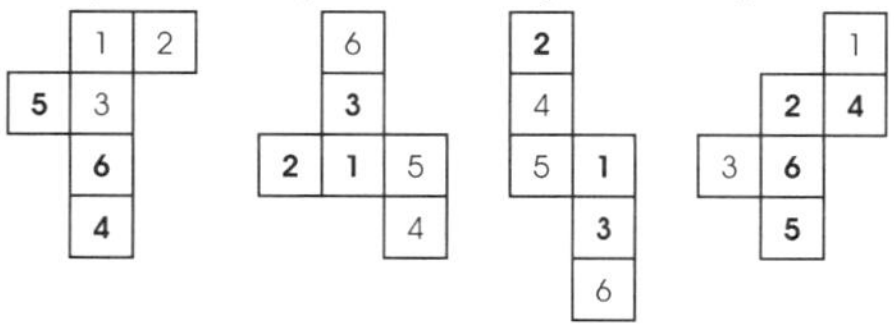

3

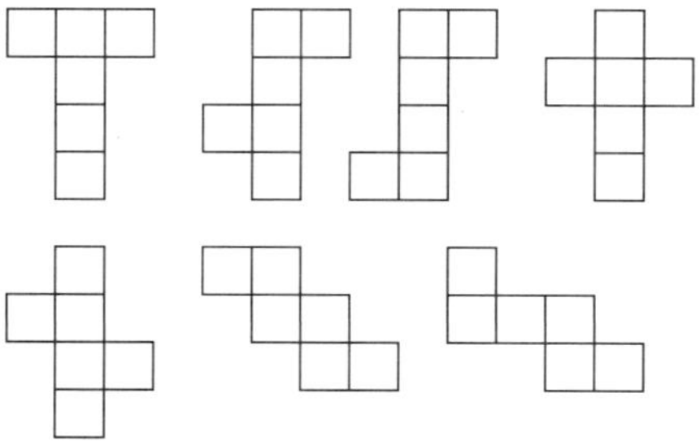

4 a) 7 faces b) 15 edges c) 10 vertices

15 Co-ordinates and shapes

On track

1 (6,1) and (2,5)
2 (2,–3) and (4,3)
3 (–6,0) (–6,4) (–2,0) (–2,4)
The square will be in the position shown here.

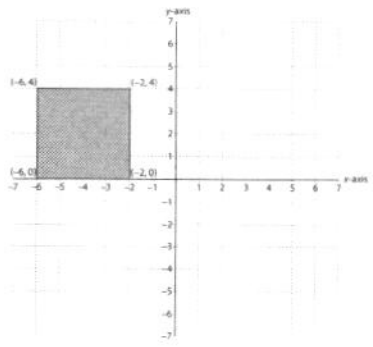

Aiming higher

1 (2,2) (6,4) (6,0)
(2,2) (6,4) (10,2)
(2,2) (10,2) (6,0)
(6,0) (6,4) (10,2)
(4,9) (8,9) (6,4)
(4,9) (8,9) (6,2)
(4,9) (8,9) (6,0)
2 a) (–6,2); (–6,4); (–2,2)
b) (2,2); (2,4); (6,2)

Using and applying

1 (0,0) (3,0) (3,–2)
2 (–3,0) (5,–2) (–1,6)

16 Measurement

On track

1 a) 1010 m 1.011 km 1100 m 1.11 km
b) 5 m 5005 mm 505 cm 5.5 m 555 cm
c) 100 ml 0.75 l 1500 ml 1.6 l 2 l
d) 1500 g 1.6 kg 2 kg 10000 g 34 kg
2 a) 875 ml b) 0.875 l
3 a) 32 kilometres b) 64 kilometres
c) 20 kilometres d) 160 kilometres
4 a) 40 miles b) 7.5 miles
c) 50 miles d) 250 miles
5 a) 240 min b) 150 min
c) 45 min d) 1440 min
6 a) 11:50 b) 15:15
c) 08:30 d) 21:20
7 a) 10:15 am b) 5:05 pm
c) 10:50 pm d) 6:00 am

Aiming higher

1 a) 200 cm 350 cm 2 cm 42.5 cm
b) 2000 g 6350 g 525 g 3175 g
c) 3.865 km 5.35 km 4.005 km 0.075 km
2 a) 13.2 lbs 22 lbs 1.1 lbs
b) 2 kg 5 kg 20 kg
3 a) 2 gallons 6 gallons 10 gallons
b) 13.5 litres 31.5 litres 90 litres
4 a) 7:15 pm b) 09:30
5 a) 2 hours 25 minutes
b) 7:40 pm c) 5:50 pm
d) 2 hours 50 minutes
e) 3:50 pm f) 9:25 pm

Using and applying

1 a) 1050 m or 1.05 km
b) 2050 m or 2.05 km
2 There are 30 lots of 8 km in 240 km, so 30 × 5 = 150 miles
3

Distance chart in miles

London				
3485	New York			
4185	7350	New Delhi		
6955	11590	3650	Tokyo	
10625	9945	6480	3025	Sydney

Distance chart in kilometres

London				
5536	New York			
6696	11760	New Delhi		
11128	18544	5840	Tokyo	
17000	15912	10368	4870	Sydney

4 a) 30 minutes
b) Bus Number 43
c) i) Bus Number 40 ii) 55 minutes
iii) 22 minutes

17 Area and perimeter

On track

1 a) 15 cm² b) 36 cm² c) 30 cm²
d) 75 cm² e) 10 cm²
2 a) 30 cm² b) 28 cm² c) 90 cm²
d) 210 cm² e) 16.5 cm²
3 a) area = 54 cm² ($\frac{1}{2}$ × 12 × 9)
b) area = 1200 cm² ($\frac{1}{2}$ × 80 × 30)
4 area = 480 cm² perimeter = 154 cm

Aiming higher

1 a) side of large square = 5 + 15 = 20 cm
area of large square = 20 × 20 = 400 cm²
b) There are four small triangles, each has an area of $\frac{1}{2}$ × 5 ×15, so the total blue area = 4 × $\frac{1}{2}$ × 5 × 15 = 150 cm²
The shaded square has an area of 400 – 150 = 250 cm²
2 a) i) 50 cm (24 cm × 1 cm),
ii) 28 cm (12 cm × 2 cm),
iii) 22 cm (8 cm × 3 cm)
iv) 20 cm (6 cm × 4 cm)
b) 74 cm (36 cm × 1 cm)
40 cm (18 cm × 2 cm)
30 cm (12 cm × 3 cm)
26 cm (9 cm × 4 cm)
24 cm (6 cm × 6 cm)
c) 9 cm² (9 cm × 1 cm)
16 cm² (8 cm × 2 cm)
21 cm² (7 cm × 3 cm)
24 cm² (6 cm × 4 cm)
25 cm² (5 cm × 5 cm)
d) 11 cm² (11 cm × 1 cm)
20 cm² (10 cm × 2 cm)
27 cm² (9 cm × 3 cm)
32 cm² (8 cm × 4 cm)
35 cm² (7 cm × 5 cm)
36 cm² (6 cm × 6 cm)
3 a) 400 cm²
The shape is made from two identical parallelograms, each with a length of 20 cm and a height of 10 cm, so 2 × 20 × 10 = 400 cm²
b) 288 cm²
The shape is made from a rectangle 24 cm × 8 cm and a triangle 24 cm × 8 cm, so (24 × 8) + ($\frac{1}{2}$ × 24 × 8) = 288 cm²

a) □ = 10 and △ = 2
These answers could be reversed

b) ⬡ = 16 and ⏢ = 2
These answers could be reversed

c) ◇ = 12 and ○ = 3

d) ◺ = 15 and ▭ = 4

Aiming higher

1 **a)** $a = 10$ **b)** $b = 10$
c) $c = 5$ **d)** $d = 150$
e) $e = 15$ **f)** $f = 10$
g) $g = 2$ **h)** $h = 2$

2 A = 7,8 B = 2,3 C = 3,4 D = 5,6

3 **a)** £7 **b)** £10 **c)** £13.50
d) £12.50 **e)** £8 **f)** £18.50
g) £12.20 **h)** £20.75

4 To find the value of ◎, you need to divide 600 by 5. This gives 120.
To find the value of ✪, first subtract the value of ◎, which you now know is 120.
So 360 – 120 = 240.
Now divide 240 by 4 to find the value of 60.
◎ = 120 ✪ = 60

Using and applying

1 **a)** 7, 10, 13 **b)** 16 squares
c) Multiply the pattern number by 3 and add 1.
d) $S = 3p + 1$
e) $S = 3 \times 35 + 1 = 106$

2 $z = 18$ $p = 50$
$c = 16$ $d = 2$

3 If package B = 6 kg, then you need three of package A to equal 6 kg, so package A must be 6 ÷ 3 = 2 kg. Package C is twice the weight of package B, so package C = 6 × 2 = 12 kg. The total weight must be 2 + 6 + 12 = 20 kg.
A = 2 kg C = 12 kg Total = 20 kg

10 Angles

On track

1 **a)** 40° **b)** 72°
2 **a)** 140° **b)** 119°
3 **a)** 35°, 145°, 145° **b)** 53°, 53°, 127°
4) **a)** Triangle 1 80° Triangle 2 47°
Triangle 3 40° Triangle 4 51°
Triangle 5 28°

Aiming higher

1 24
2 A = 110° B = 65° C = 110°
3 **a)** 125°, 55°, 55°
b) 62°
4 Quadrilateral 1 150°
Quadrilateral 2 176°
Quadrilateral 3 96°
Quadrilateral 4 121°
Quadrilateral 5 218°

Using and applying

1 210° or 150°
Explanation, e.g. 12 hours is 360°, so 1 hour is 30° (360 ÷ 12), so 7 hours is 210°, or if you look at the other angle, 5 hours is 150°

2 Between 15° and 25°

3 23°, 37°, 120°
Explanation: Starting with the given angle of 67° and the 90° of the square, the left angle of the triangle must be 180 – (67 + 90) = 23°. Then moving to the equilateral triangle, all angles must be 60° (180 ÷ 3), so the obtuse angle in the shaded triangle must be 180 – 60 = 120°. The third angle of the shaded triangle will be 180 – (23 + 120) = 37°

4

Regular shape	Create triangles	Sum of interior angles (°)	Size of each interior angle (°)
Triangle Number of sides: 3	Number of triangles: 1	**180** × 1 = 180	**180** ÷ 3 = 60
Quadrilateral (Square) Number of sides: **4**	Number of triangles: **2**	**180 × 2 = 360**	**360** ÷ 4 = 90
Pentagon Number of sides: **5**	Number of triangles: **3**	**180 × 3 = 540**	**540** ÷ 5 = **108**

b) There are a number of patterns.
E.g. the numbers in the first two columns increase by 1 and in the third the totals increase by 180.
The key pattern is the number of triangles is always two less than the number of sides of the shape. You will need this to help you calculate the answer to c) more quickly.

c) Using the idea that the number of interior triangles is always two less than the number of sides, it is possible to calculate the size of the interior angles
i) Regular heptagon: about 128.57°
(7 – 2) × 180 = 900
900 ÷ 7 is about 128.57
ii) Regular octagon: 135°
(8 – 2) × 180 = 1080
1080 ÷ 8 = 135

11 2-D shapes

On track

1 **a)** rectangle (or oblong)/irregular
b) hexagon/regular
c) parallelogram/irregular
d) rhombus (not diamond)/irregular
e) hexagon/irregular
f) octagon/irregular

2 **a)** 0 right angles, D
b) 1 right angle, A, E
c) 2 right angles, B
d) 3 right angles, C, F

3 A, E, F

4 A, C, D

Aiming higher

1 **A a)** equilateral **b)** acute-angled
B a) isosceles **b)** acute-angled
C a) scalene **b)** right-angled
D a) scalene **b)** obtuse-angled
E a) isosceles **b)** right-angled
F a) isosceles **b)** obtuse-angled
G a) scalene **b)** acute-angled
An equilateral triangle not only has three equal sides but also has three equal angles, so 180 ÷ 3 = 60, the angles of an equilateral triangle are always 60°.

2 9 cm and 11 cm

3 **a)** A B, G, F
b) C and D, H and I

4 **a)** square
b) rectangle (or oblong)
c) parallelogram
d) kite

Using and applying

1 **a)** A decagon (10 sided-shape)
b) octagon (8-sided shape)
c) quadrilateral (4-sided shape) or other special quadrilateral
d) triangle (3-sided shape)
e) Heptagon (7-sided shape)

2 **a)** 30 squares
b) The totals for the different-sized squares are the square numbers up to 4:
1 + 4 + 9 + 16 = 30
c) 55 squares
d) i) 13 triangles
ii) No, the pattern of square numbers does not apply here

3 **a)** a regular pentagon
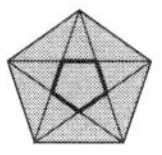

b) a rhombus
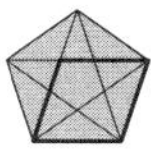

c) a kite
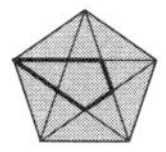

d) two different trapeziums
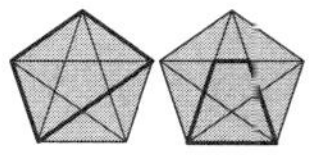

e) **three** different isosceles triangles
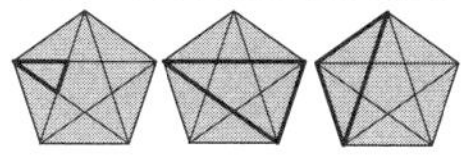

12 Circles

On track

1 **a)** B **b)** A **c)** C
2 **a)** 10 cm **b)** 32 cm **c)** 17 cm
d) 54 cm **e)** 71 cm
3 **a)** 7 cm **b)** 27 cm **c)** 11.5 cm
d) 2.25 cm **e)** 125 cm
4 4000 times
5 75 m
6 **a)** 24 cm **b)** 35 cm
c) 1.5 cm **d)** 10.5 cm
7 **a)** To find the radius you have to divide the diameter by 2.
b) $r = \frac{1}{2}\frac{D}{2}$

Aiming higher

1 12.5 m
2 11.6 m
3 7.5 cm – the circumference of the circle touches the sides of the square, so the diameter of the circle is the same as the side of a square.

Using and applying

1 **a)** length = 72 cm width = 48 cm
The length of the rectangle is six radiuses and the width is four radiuses.
b) length = 45 cm width = 18 cm
The length of the rectangle is two and a half diameters and width one diameter.
c) length = 48 cm
The rectangle is four circles long. There are three circle in the upper row and 6 cm at either end, so that makes three circles + 12 cm, so the diameter of each circle is 12 cm.

2 18 cm
The radius of the largest circle is 5 + 2 + 2 = 9 cm, so the diameter is 18 cm (9 × 2).

3 The circumference is a little more than 3 times the diameter. If you worked it out to be 3.1 or 3.2, well done.

13 3-D solids

On track

1 6 faces, 12 edges, 8 vertices
2 **a)** 3 cuboids of increasing size
b) 8 **c)** 16
3 **a)** cuboid
b) tetrahedron or triangular-based pyramid
c) cylinder **d)** cube
4 **a)** B, D, F **b)** A, C, E, **c)** A, B, D, F
d) E, F **e)** A, C, E

Aiming higher

1 **a)** triangular prism
b) yes, the triangular faces are parallel
c) yes, the triangular face and the base rectangle are perpendicular
2 **a)** a triangular-based pyramid (or tetrahedron)
b) the base and one other triangular face could be perpendicular
c) no
3 **a)** cylinder **b)** cuboid
c) cube **d)** sphere
4 8

Key facts

Angles in a **triangle** add up to 180°.
Angles on a **straight line** add up to 180°.
Angles around a point add up to 360°.
Angles in an **equilateral triangle** each measure 60°.
Two angles in an isosceles triangle are equal: these are the angles opposite the equal sides.
Angles in a quadrilateral add up to 360°.
Vertically opposite angles are equal.

Language

Perpendicular lines are at right angles to each other
Vertical lines are **perpendicular** to **horizontal** lines
Interior angle the inside angle of a shape

On track

1 a) Calculate the size of the third angle in the triangle.

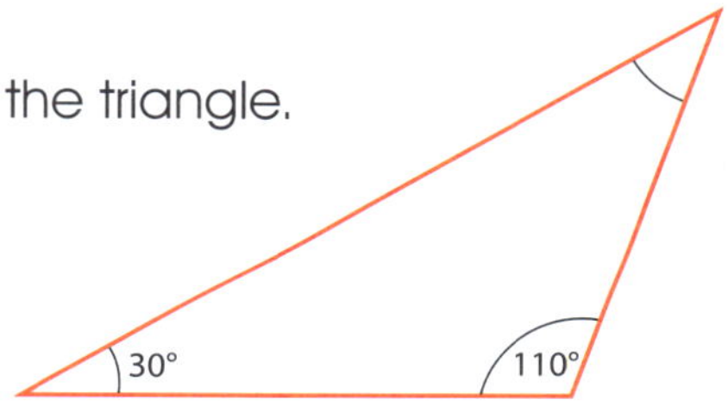

b) Calculate the missing angles in this isosceles triangle.

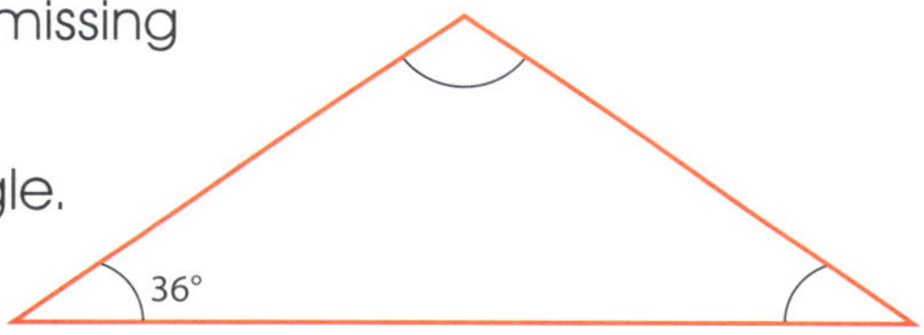

2 a) Calculate the size of the fourth angle in the quadrilateral.

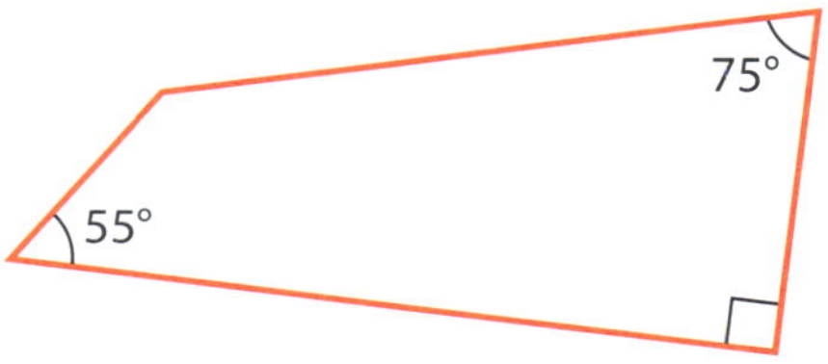

b) Calculate the missing angle in this quadrilateral.

3 **a)** These two straight lines cross. You have been given one angle. Calculate the other three angles.

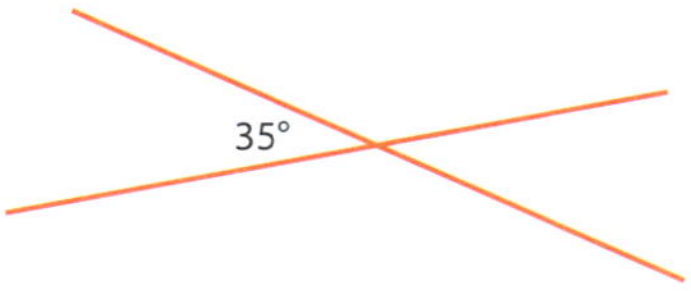

b) These two straight lines cross. You have been given one angle. Calculate the other three angles.

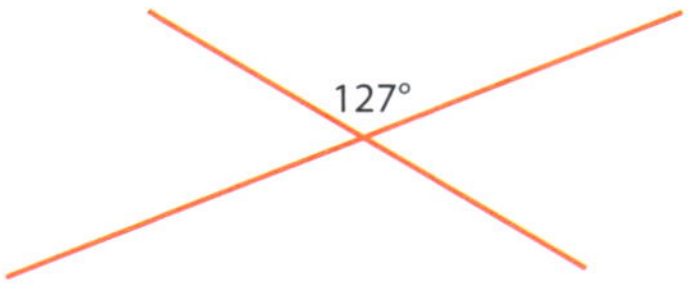

4 This table shows the angles of five triangles.

Use the formula: $a = 180 - (b + c)$ to find the missing angle, where b and c are the known angles.

	a	*b*	*c*
Triangle 1		45°	55°
Triangle 2		60°	73°
Triangle 3		15°	125°
Triangle 4		105°	24°
Triangle 5		69°	83°

Aiming higher

1 There are a number of equal angles around a point. The size of each angle is 15°. How many equal angles are there?

2 These three triangles are all isosceles triangles. Find the value of angles A, B and C.

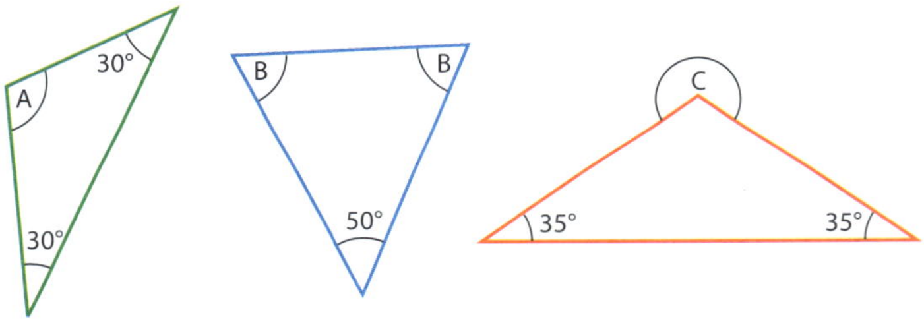

3 **a)** This shape is a parallelogram. Find the three missing angles.

b) This shape is a right-angled triangle. Find the third angle.

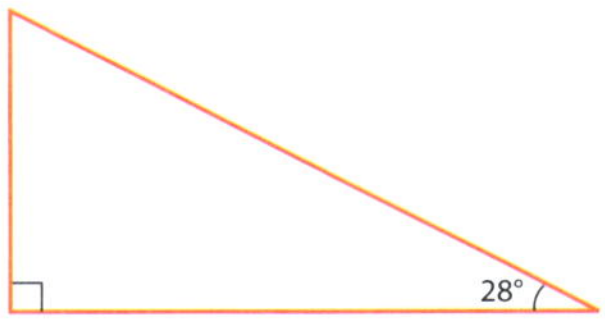

4 This table shows the angles of five quadrilaterals.

Use the formula: $a = 360 - (b + c + d)$ to find the missing angle, where *b*, *c* and *d* are the known angles.

	a	*b*	*c*	*d*
Quadrilateral 1		35°	65°	110°
Quadrilateral 2		22°	95°	67°
Quadrilateral 3		82°	134°	48°
Quadrilateral 4		140°	23°	76°
Quadrilateral 5		38°	48°	56°

Using and applying

1 What are the possible angles between the hands of a clock at seven o'clock?
Explain how you know.

2 For safety the angle between a ladder and the ground must be between 65° and 75°. Between what values must the angle between the ladder and the wall be?

3 A square and an equilateral triangle are on a straight line.

They form a shaded triangle.

Find the angles of the shaded triangle.

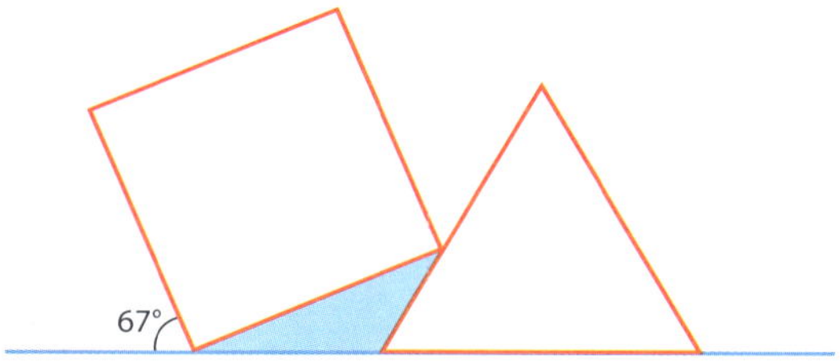

4 This table will help to calculate the size of interior angles of regular polygons.

a) Copy and complete the table.

Regular shape	Create triangles	Sum of interior angles	Size of each interior angle
Triangle 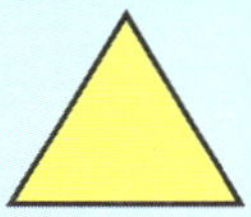 Number of sides: 3	Number of triangles: 1 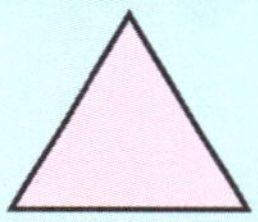	180° × 1 = 180°	180° ÷ 3 = 60°
Quadrilateral (Square)  Number of sides: __	Number of triangles: __ 	180° × __ = __°	360° ÷ 4 = 90°
Pentagon 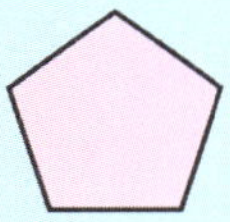 Number of sides: __	Number of triangles: __ 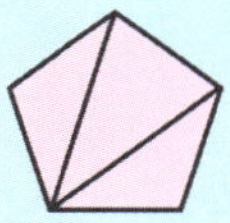	180° × __ = __°	__° ÷ __ = __°

a) Describe any patterns you can find.

b) Calculate the interior angle of:

i) a regular heptagon (seven-sided shape)

ii) a regular octagon (eight-sided shape).

11 2-D shapes

What will you learn?

How to:

- compare and classify geometric shapes based on their properties and sizes.

I need to be able to:

- state and use the properties of a rectangle (including squares) to deduce related facts.

Examples

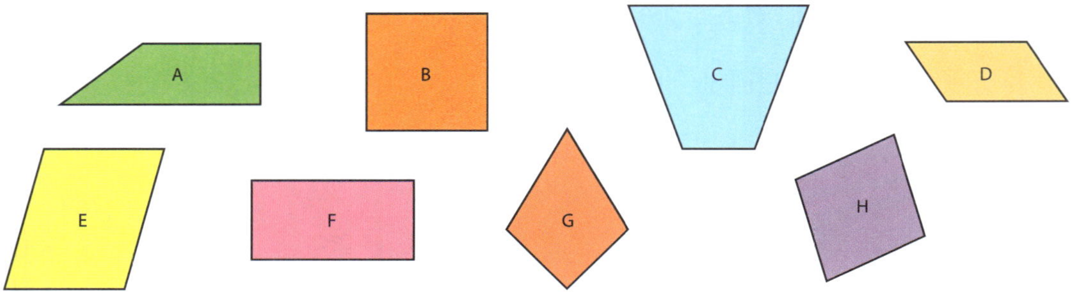

1 Which of these quadrilaterals is a:

square?	rectangle?	kite?	parallelogram?	trapezium?	rhombus?
B	*F*	*G*	*D, E*	*A, C*	*H*

2 Which of the quadrilaterals have two pairs of parallel lines?

A, B, D, E, H have two pairs of parallel lines.

Key facts

Regular A shape with all its sides equal in length and all its angles equal in size.

Irregular A shape that does not have its sides equal in length and the angles are not the same size.

Vertex (plural **vertices**) a corner on a 2-D shape

Side a line joining two vertices on a 2-D shape

Diagonal a straight line drawn from one non-adjacent vertex of a shape to another vertex

Quadrilateral a 2-D shape with four straight sides

Parallel lines remain the same distance apart along all of their length

Perpendicular lines are at right angles to each other

On track

1 Name these shapes and say whether they are regular or irregular:

Hint: Some of these shapes are quadrilaterals. Can you be more specific with their names?

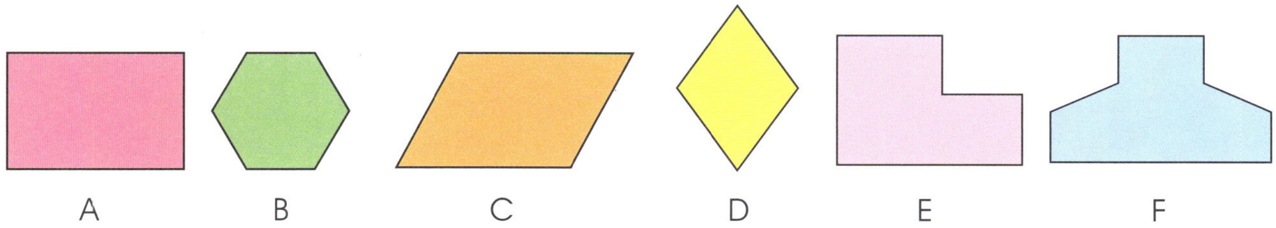

2

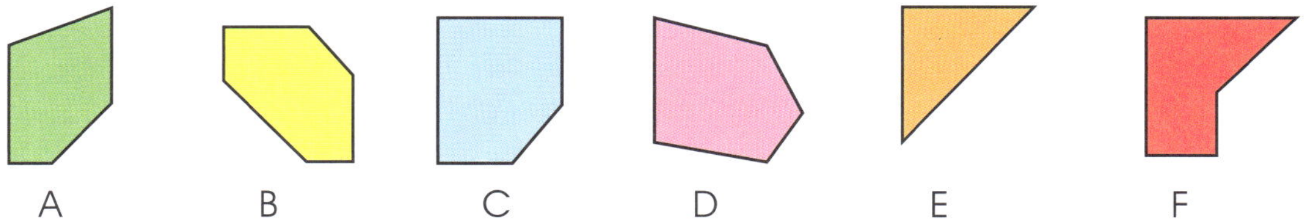

List the shapes that have:

a) 0 right angles **b)** 1 right angles

c) 2 right angles **d)** 3 right angles.

3 Trapeziums are **quadrilaterals** with **one** pair of parallel lines.

Which of these shapes are trapeziums?

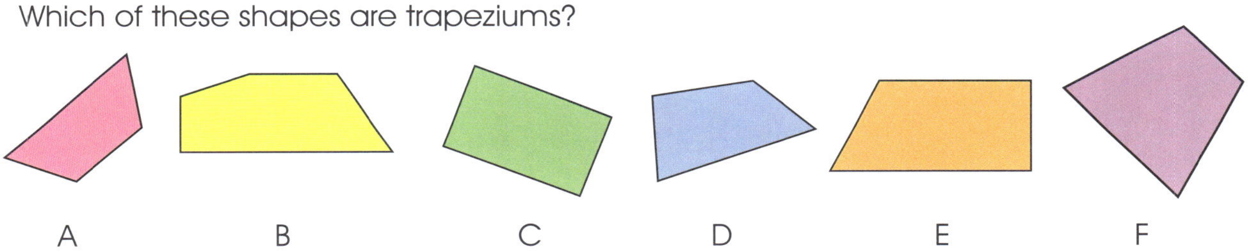

4 List the **regular** shapes.

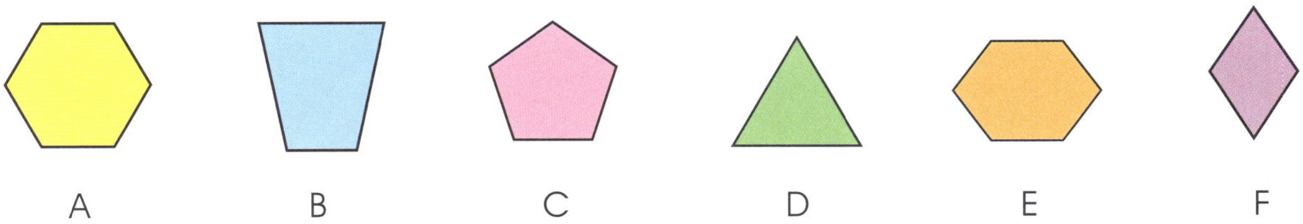

Aiming higher

1 Triangles can all be given two names.

If they are named by their sides, they can be equilateral, isosceles or scalene.
If they are named by their angles, they can be acute-angle, right-angled or obtuse-angled.

Name each of these triangles by:

a) its sides **b)** its angles.

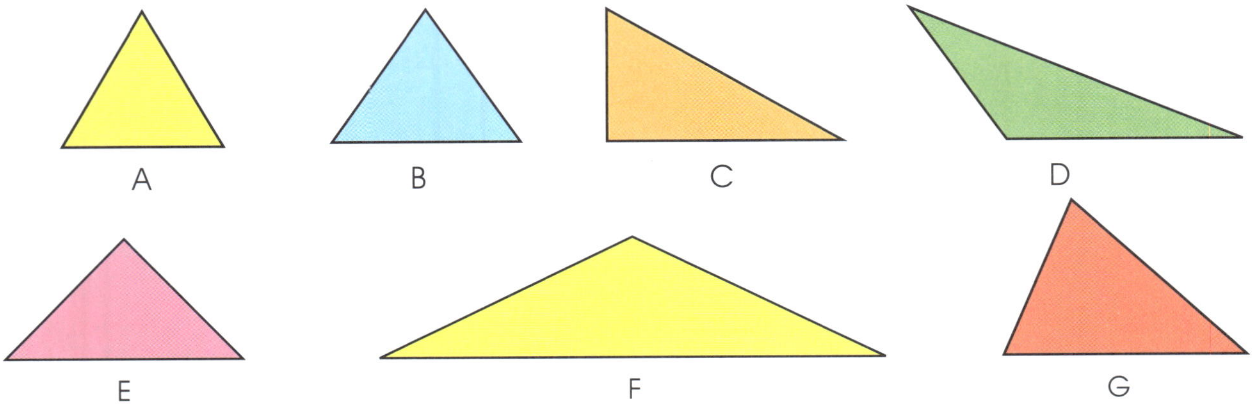

2 You are going to draw a triangle. You will need some plain paper.

Draw a line, AB, of 10 cm.

Use a protractor or angle measurer to draw two angles; one at A of 50° and one at B of 70°.

Construct the triangle.

How long are the other two sides to the nearest whole centimetre?

3 Look at the diagram opposite.

a) Which four triangles in the diagram together make a kite?

b) Write down a pair of triangles that will make a parallelogram.

Can you find a different pair?

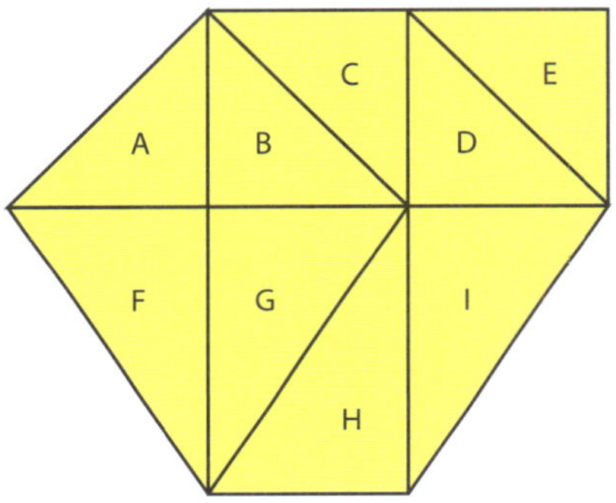

4 These are the **diagonals** of quadrilaterals.

Name the quadrilaterals.

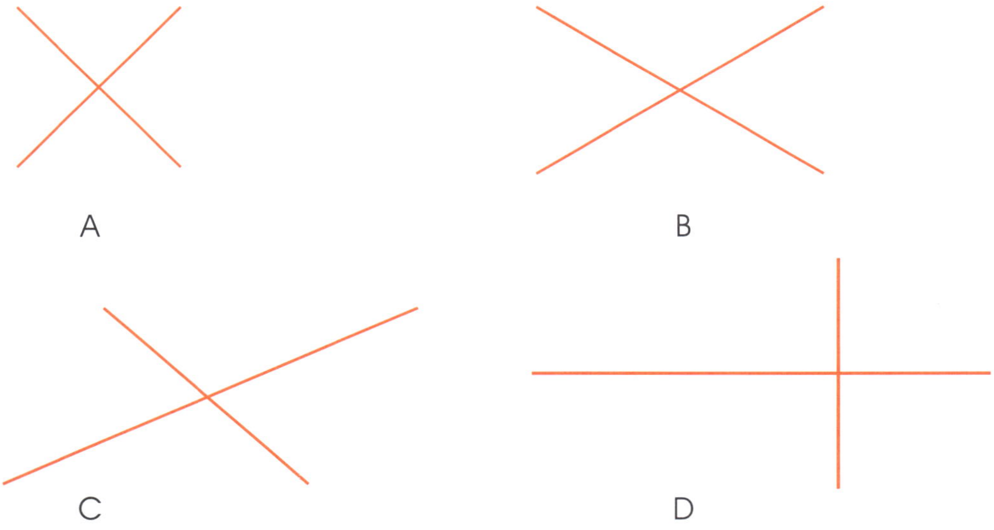

Using and applying

1 This grid has the names of some polygons.

hexagon	A	triangle	19
B	C	quadrilateral	16
pentagon	D	E	15
19	17	14	

The number at the end of each row and at the bottom of each column shows the number of sides the shapes in that row or column have.

Give possible names for shapes A – E.

A: __________ B: __________ C: __________ D: __________ E: __________

2 a) How many squares can you find here?

b) Can you find a pattern using squares of different sizes?

(Clue: Some squares are 3×3, some are 2×2 and so on.)

c) Use this pattern to help you calculate the number of squares in a five-by-five grid.

d) i) How many triangles can you find here?

ii) Can you use the same pattern work with triangles?

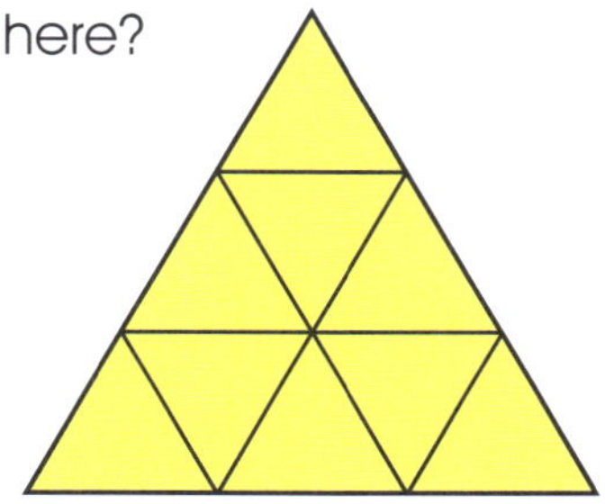

3 Can you find these shapes inside the regular pentagon?

a) A regular pentagon

b) A rhombus

c) A kite

d) Two different trapeziums

e) Three different isosceles triangles

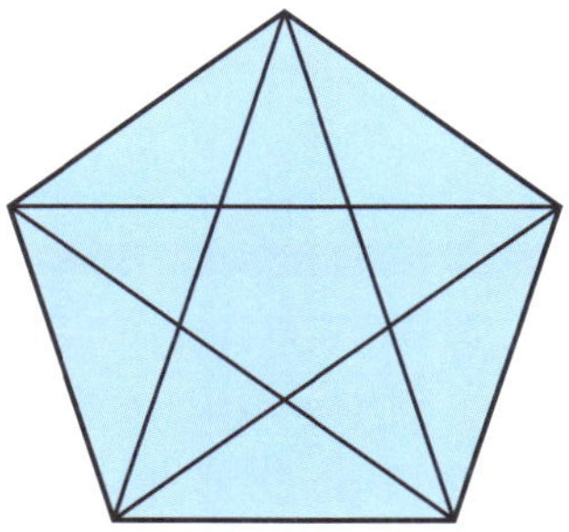

12 Circles

What will you learn?

How to:

- illustrate and name parts of circles including radius, diameter and circumference.

I need to be able to:

- multiply and divide numbers mentally, drawing upon known facts
- double and halve numbers.

Example

A circle has a diameter of 12 cm.
What is the radius of the circle?

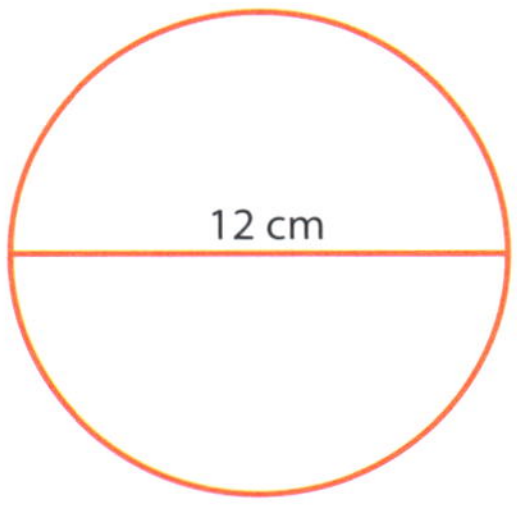

6 cm

The radius is half of the diameter: 12 ÷ 2 = 6.

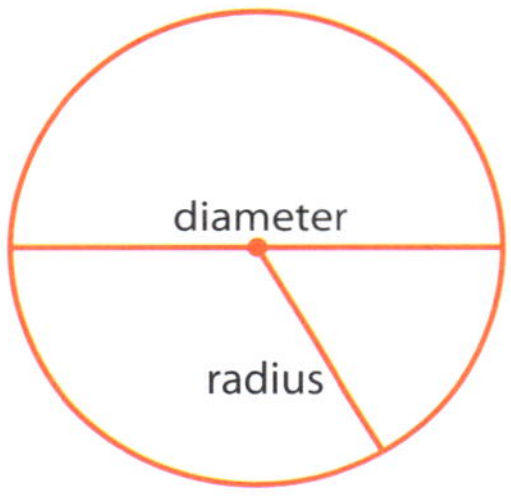

Key facts

A diameter is a straight line that must pass through the centre of a circle.
A radius is the distance from the centre of a circle to the circumference.
A diameter is made up from radii.

Language

Circumference the distance around the outside of a circle

Diameter the shortest distance through the centre of a circle joining two opposite points on the edge of the circle

Radius the shortest distance from the centre of a circle to the edge

On track

1 Each circle has a dotted line.

Which circle has a dotted line that is

a) a circumference

b) a diameter

c) a radius?

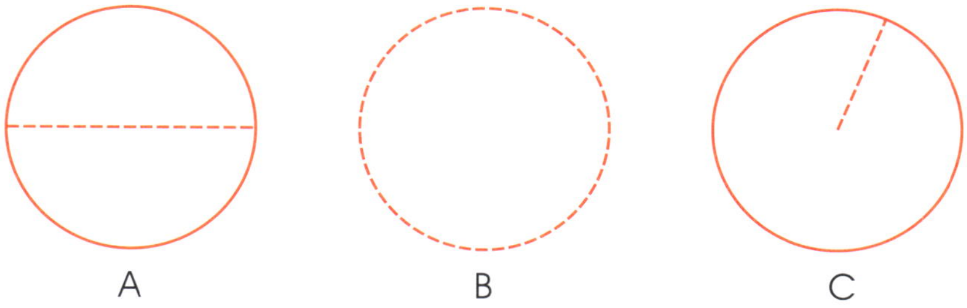

2 Here is a table of radiuses of some circles.

Calculate the diameters of each circle.

	Radius (in cm)	Diameter (in cm)
a)	5 cm	
b)	16 cm	
c)	8.5 cm	
d)	27 cm	
e)	35.5 cm	

3 Here is a table of diameters of some circles.

Calculate the radiuses of each circle.

	Diameter (in cm)	Radius (in cm)
a)	14 cm	
b)	54 cm	
c)	23 cm	
d)	4.5 cm	
e)	250 cm	

4 The circumference of the wheel of a lorry is 3 m.

How many times will the wheel turn if the lorry travels 12 km?

5 An arena is made up of two identical semi-circles and two straight sections.

The distance along the straight section is 150 m.

The distance around the whole arena is 450 m.

What is the length of the curved part of one semi-circle?

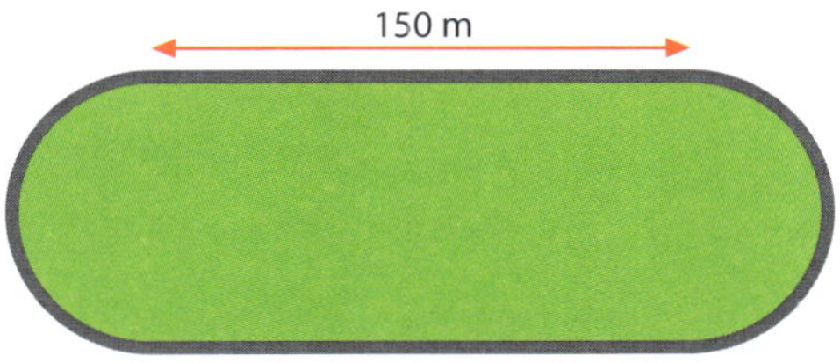

6 The formula for finding the diameter of a circle is $D = 2r$

Use the formula to find the diameter of a circle when $r =$

a) 12 cm **b)** 17.5 cm **c)** 0.75 cm **d)** 5.25 cm

7 The formula for finding the diameter of a circle is $D = 2r$

a) Explain how to find the radius of a circle when the diameter is known.

b) Write this explanation as a formula, beginning with $r =$

Aiming higher

1 There is a pond in the garden at a country house. In the centre of the pond is a fountain.

The pond is 25 m across.

How far is it from the centre of the fountain to the edge of the pond?

2 A gardener is making a circular lawn. He puts a bird bath in the centre.

From the centre of the bird bath to the edge of the lawn is 5.8 m.

How far across the whole lawn is it?

3 This is a 15 cm square.

What is the radius of the circle?

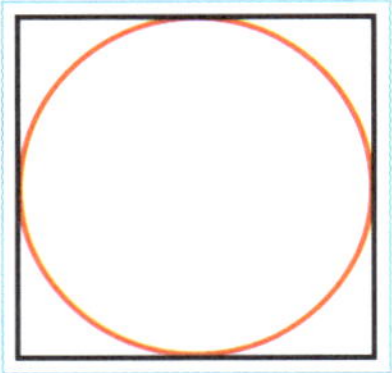

Using and applying

1 **a)** This design is made up from six circles, each with a radius of 12 cm, and a rectangle.

How long and wide is the rectangle?

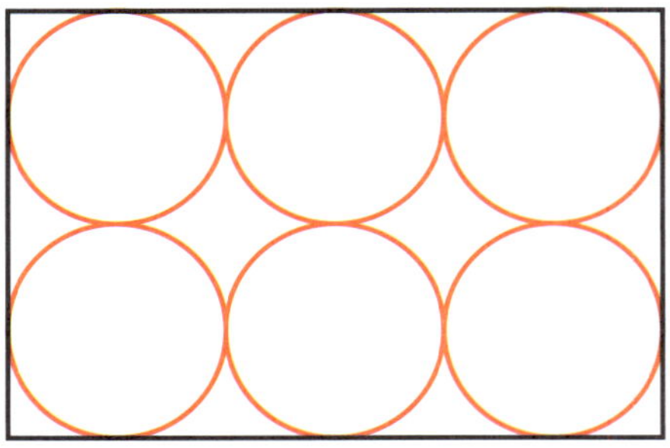

b) Here are four intersecting circles, each circle with a diameter of 18 cm.

How long and wide is the rectangle?

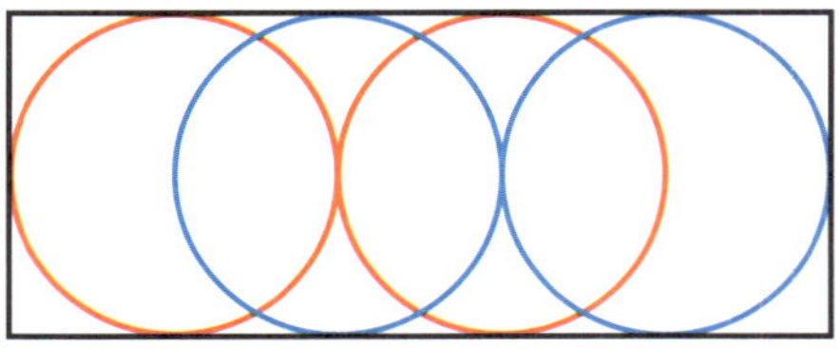

c) This design is made up of 7 identical circles and a rectangle.

The distance shown by the double-headed arrow is 6 cm.

How long is the rectangle?

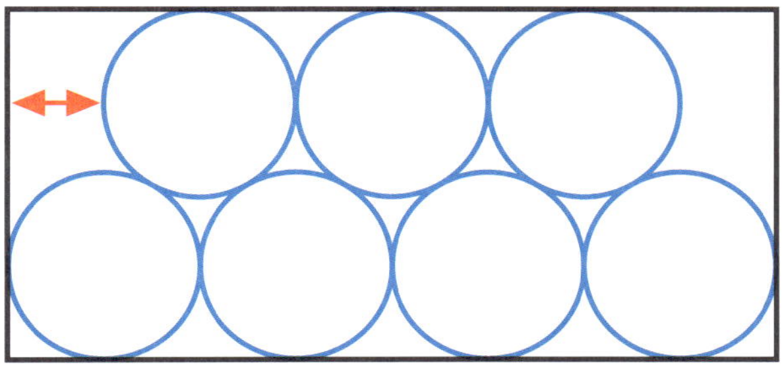

2 Here are three circles with the same centre.

The radius of the small circle is 5 cm.

The gap between each pair of circumferences is 2 cm.

What is the diameter of the largest circle?

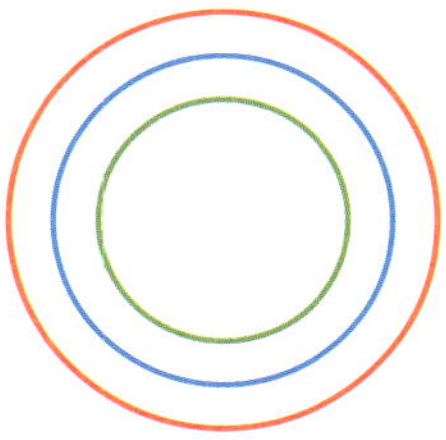

3 **Investigation**

Draw some circles of different sizes.

Measure the circumference and the diameter. You might want to use a piece of string to do this and then measure the string.

What do you notice about the two distances for each circle?

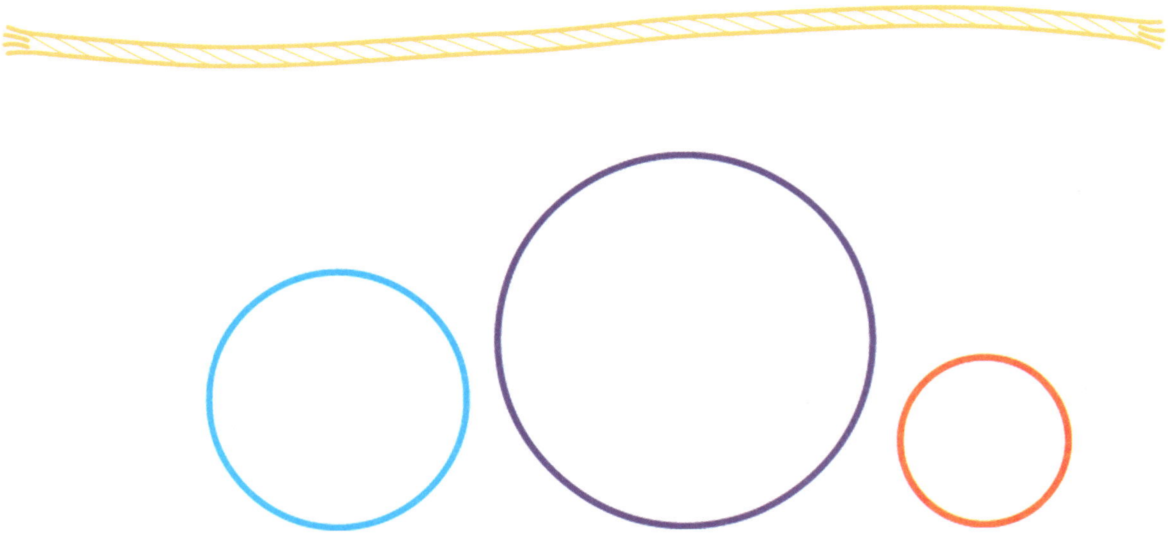

13 3-D solids

What will you learn?

How to:

- describe properties of simple 3-D shapes.

I need to be able to:

- distinguish between regular and irregular polygons based on reasoning about equal sides and angles.

Example

How many faces, edges and vertices does an octagonal prism have?

- *10 faces, 24 edges and 16 vertices*

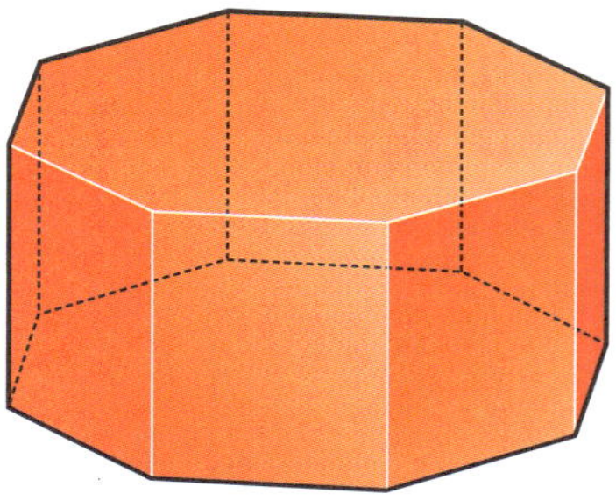

Key facts

This is a **cuboid**.

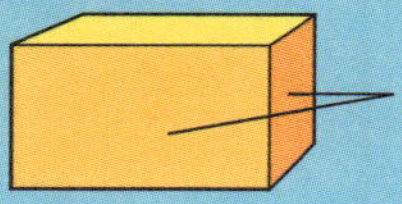

This is a **cube**.

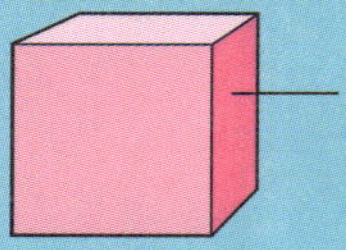

Prisms are solids that have a cross-section that is the same all the way through the shape; the two end faces are the same as the vertical cross-section. A cuboid is a type of prism.

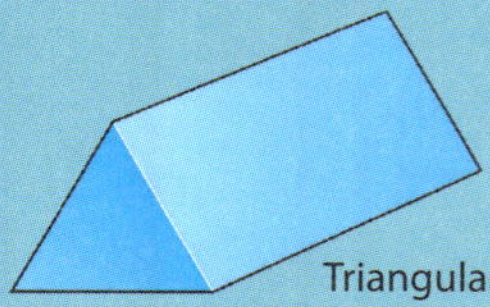

Pyramids are solids with a base and other sides that come to one vertex; this vertex is sometimes called the apex. The base can be any 2-D shape; all other faces will be triangles.

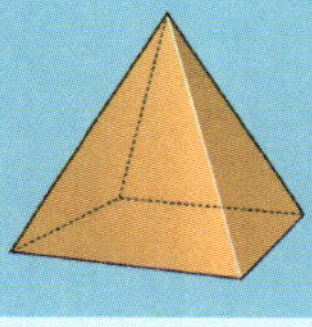

Language

Face a flat side of a 3-D solid

Edge the boundary between two faces on a 3-D solid

Vertex (plural **vertices**) a corner on a 3-D solid

Parallel faces remain the same distance apart along all of their dimensions

Perpendicular faces are at right angles to each other

On track

1 How many faces, edges and vertices does a cuboid have?

2 This picture shows a set of steps.

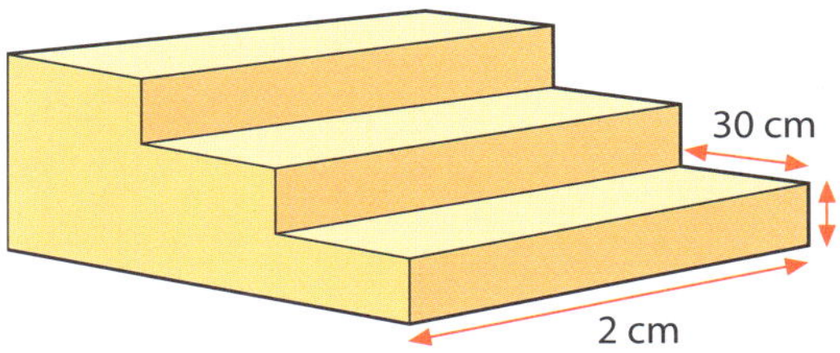

a) What solid shapes could they be made from?

b) How many vertical edges are there?

c) How many horizontal edges are there?

3 Use the clues to identify the solids.

a) I have 6 faces.
Each face is a rectangle.
What solid am I?

b) I have 4 faces.
Each face is a triangle.
What solid am I?

c) I have 3 faces.
One of my faces is rectangular, but curved.
What solid am I?

d) I have 3 pairs of parallel faces.
Each edge is the same length.
What solid am I?

4

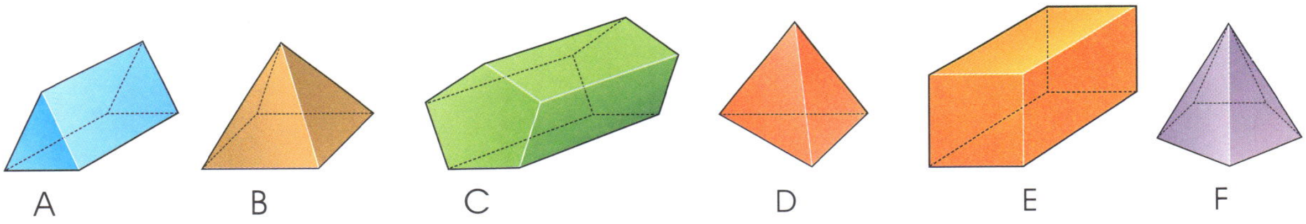

a) Which of the above are pyramids?

b) Which of the solids above are prisms?

c) Which of the solids above have at least one triangular face?

d) Which of the solids above have exactly six faces?

e) Which of the solids above have at least one pair of faces that are parallel?

Aiming higher

1 a) Name this solid.

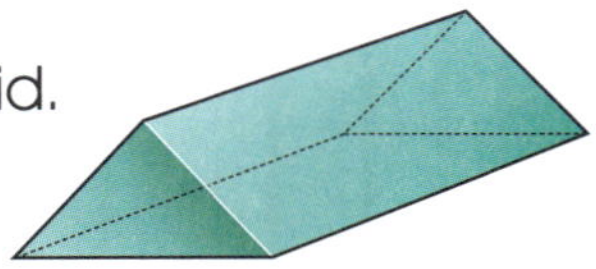

b) Could it have any parallel faces?

c) Could it have any perpendicular faces?

2 a) Name this solid.

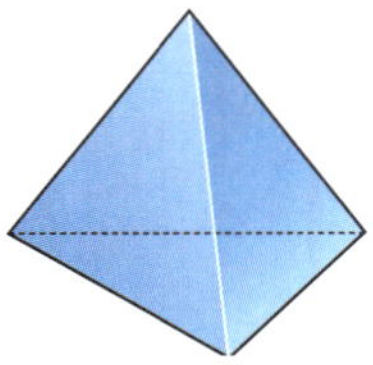

b) Could it have any perpendicular faces?

c) This solid as drawn doesn't have any parallel faces, but is it possible for this type of solid to have any parallel faces?

3 In real life, what mathematical name would you give to:

a) a can of beans

b) a box of breakfast cereal

c) a dice

d) a football?

4 Here are two square-based pyramids. They are both exactly the same size.

If you joined them by fitting the square faces together, how many faces would your new shape have?

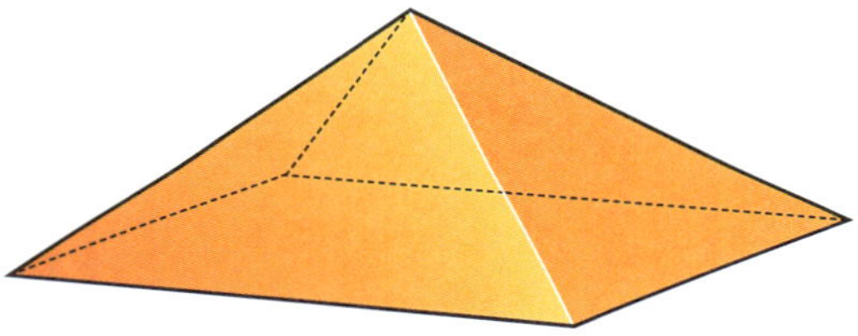

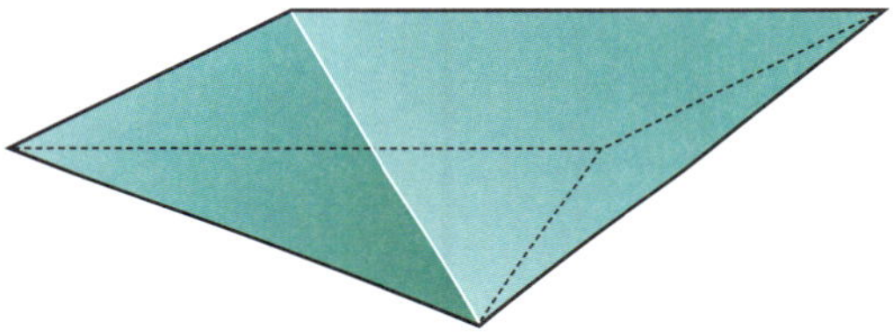

Using and applying

1 A square-based pyramid has five faces and five vertices.

a) How many faces and vertices does a pyramid with a three-sided (triangular) base have? Do you know another name for pyramids with a triangular base?

b) How many faces and vertices does a pyramid with a five-sided base have?

c) Can you find a connection between the number of faces and vertices in a pyramid and the number of sides of its base?

2 **a)** Copy and complete this table showing the number of faces, edges and vertices for the named prisms.

	Faces	Edges	Vertices
Triangular prism			
Rectangular prism			
Pentagonal prism			

b) Describe any patterns you can find in the table.

c) Use the patterns to predict how many faces, edges and vertices there will be in:

i) an octagonal prism

ii) a icosagonal prism.

Hint: An icosagon has 20 sides.

3 Here is a larger cuboid.

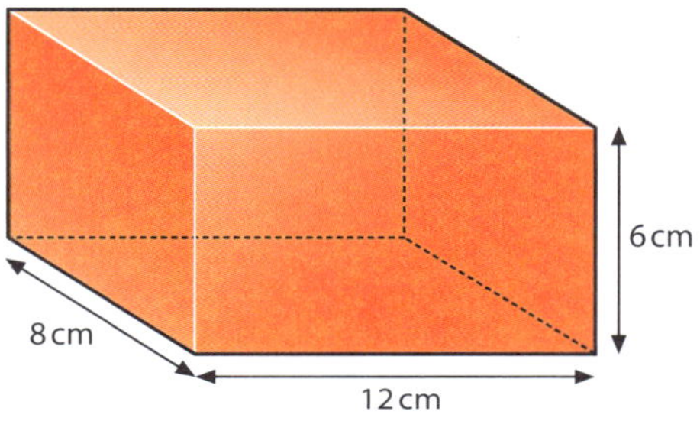

Here is a smaller cuboid.

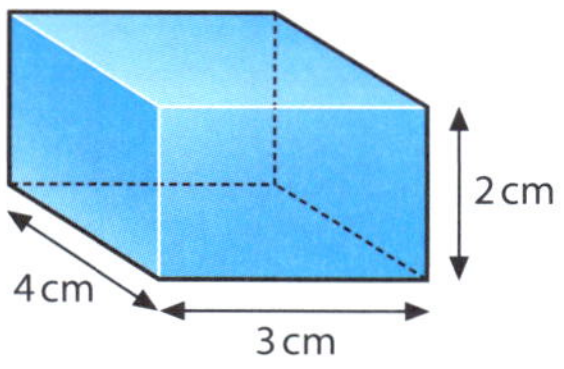

How many of the smaller cuboids will fit inside the larger cuboid?

4 You will need some interlocking cubes.

If you don't have any interlocking cubes you could draw the cuboid instead.

Make a cuboid that shows these faces:

A

B

C

14 Nets of solids

What will you learn?

How to:

- recognise, describe and build simple 3-D shapes, including making nets.

I need to be able to:

- identify 3-D shapes including cubes and cuboids from 2-D representations.

Example

This is a square-based pyramid.

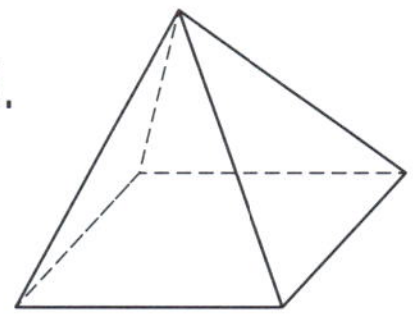

Which of these nets will make a square-based pyramid?

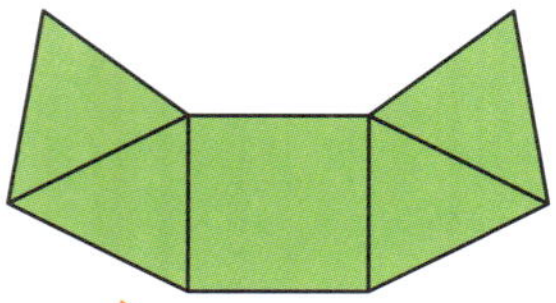

a)

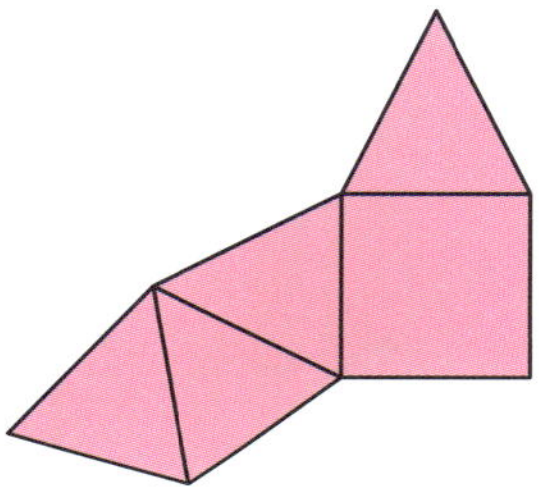

b)

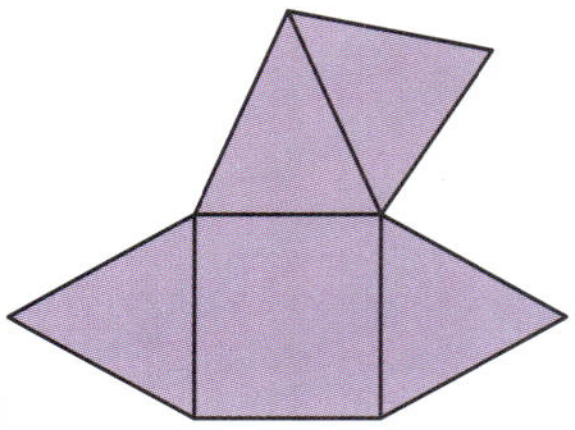

c)

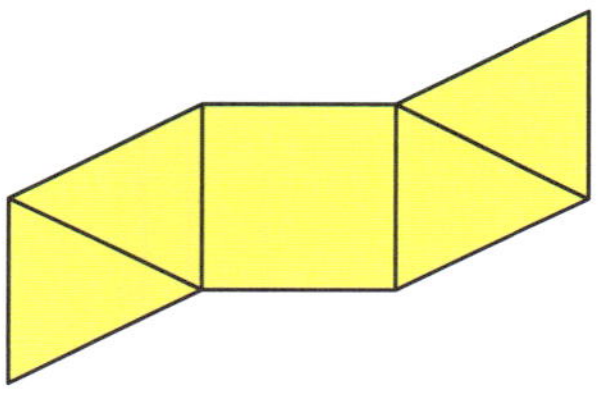

d)

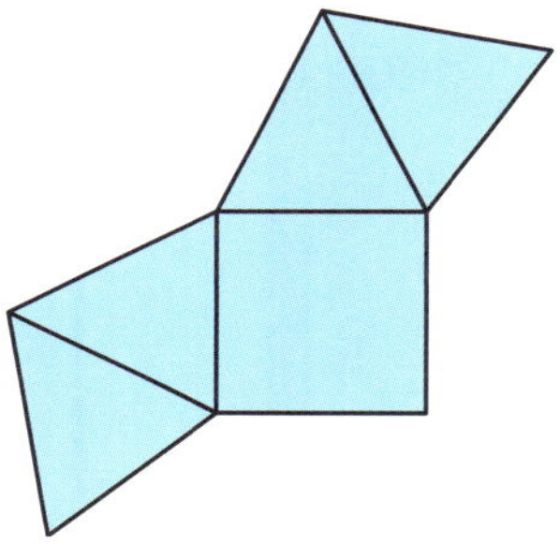

e)

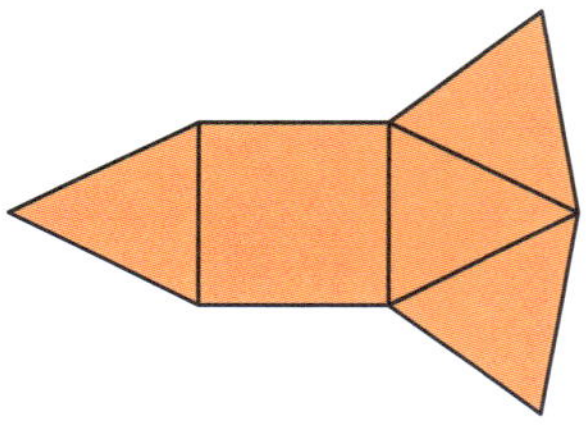

f)

Answer: b, d, e, f

Key fact

The 2-D net of a 3-D shape will fold up to make the 3-D shape.

Language

Net the faces of a 3-D solid opened out and laid flat

On track

1 Copy the diagram onto dotty or squared paper.

Add two more squares to complete a net for a cube.

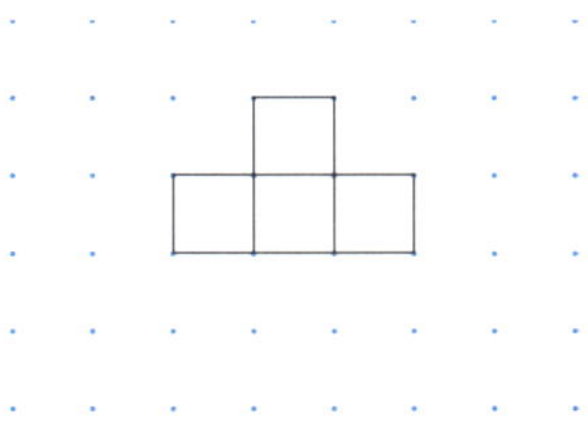

2 Copy and complete this sentence by adding the name of a 2-D shape:

a) Each face of a cuboid will be a _____.

b) A triangular prism will have two faces that are _____ and three faces that are _____.

c) A square-based pyramid will have one face that is a _____ and four faces that are _____.

d) A tetrahedron will have four faces that are _____.

3 Name the solids that are made from these nets.

a)

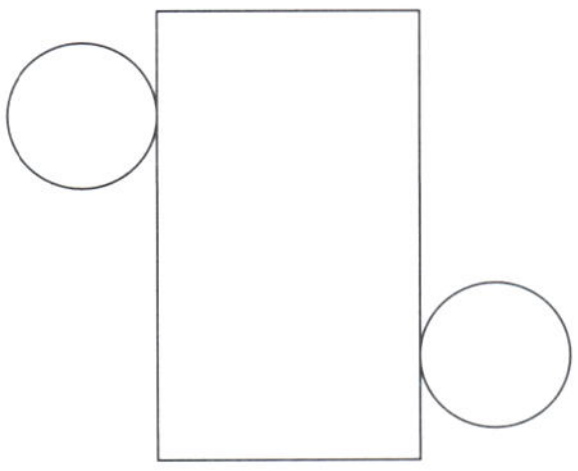

b)

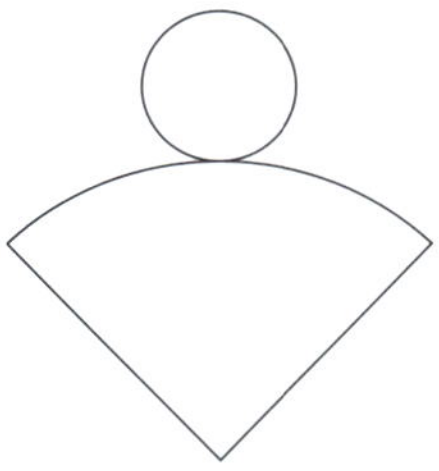

4 On centimetre squared paper, draw the net of a cuboid using the measurements shown.

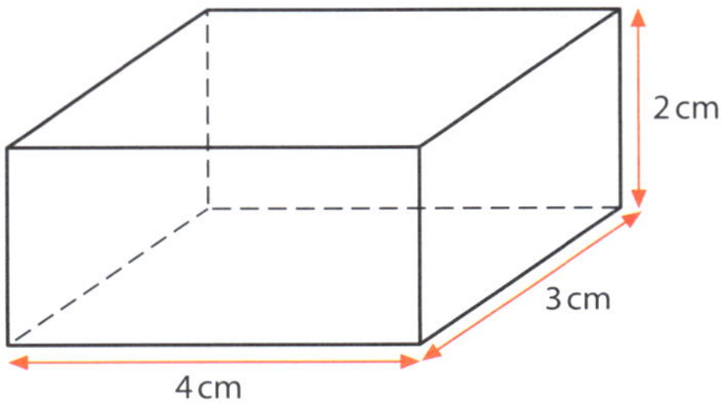

Aiming higher

1 These are nets. Name the 3-D solids they will make.

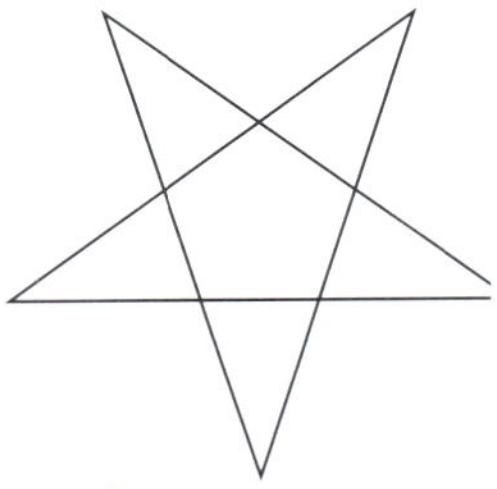

a)

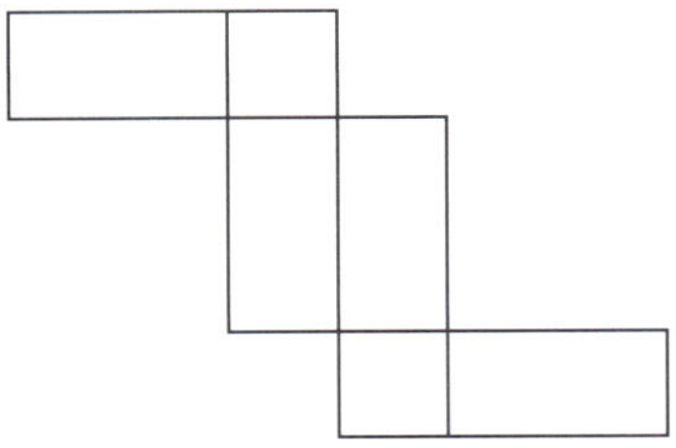

b)

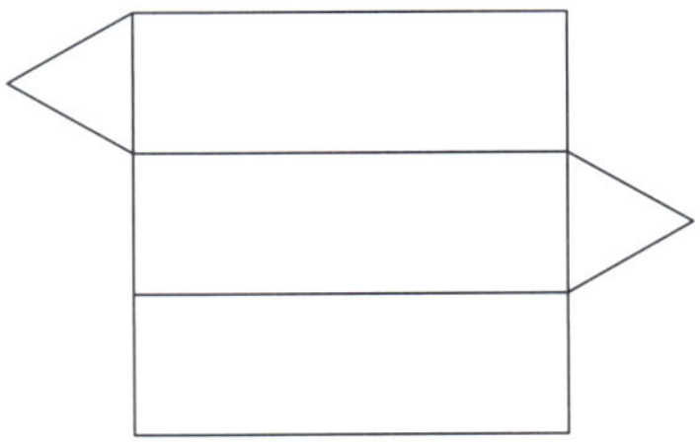

c)

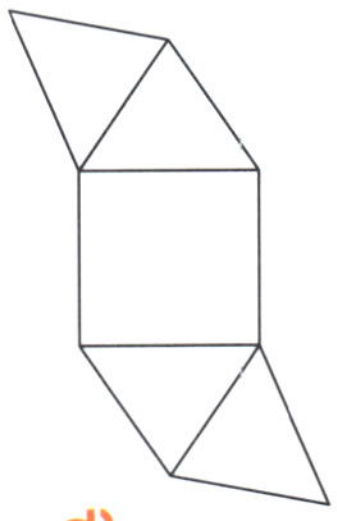

d)

2 Which of these drawings are nets for a tetrahedron?

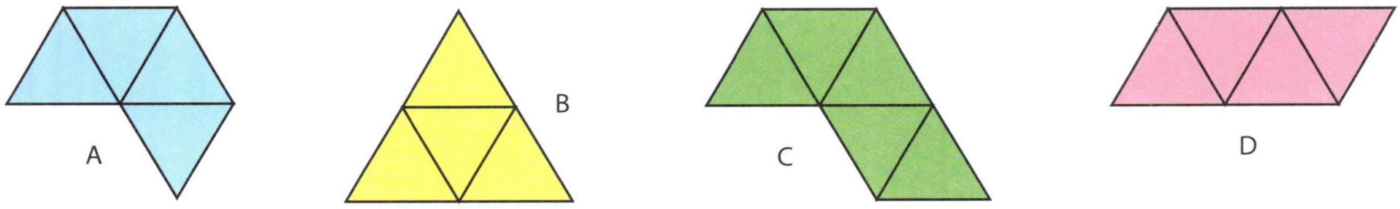

3 These are nets of an open cube. They show the base marked B and four sides.

The sides of the cube are all marked with a horizontal stripe; one is marked for you.

Copy the nets and draw the horizontal stripe on the other three sides.

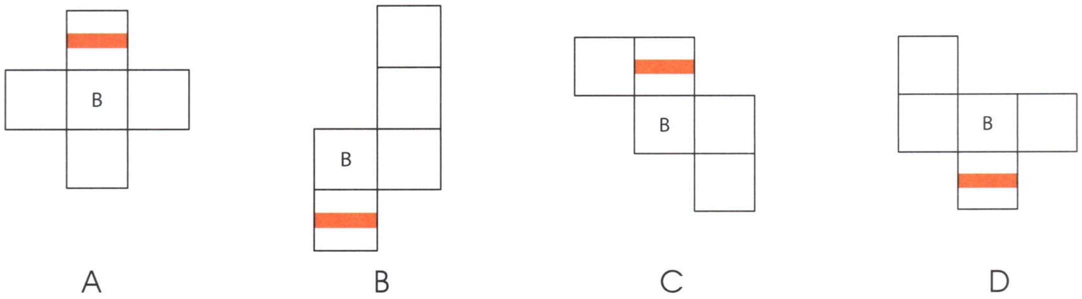

4 Answer 'true' or 'false' to these statements.

a) A triangular based pyramid can use scalene triangles.

b) A cuboid can have four square faces and two rectangular faces.

c) A hexagonal prism must have six rectangular faces.

d) The triangular faces of a tetrahedron must be equilateral triangles.

Using and applying

1 Which of these drawings are nets for a square-based pyramid?

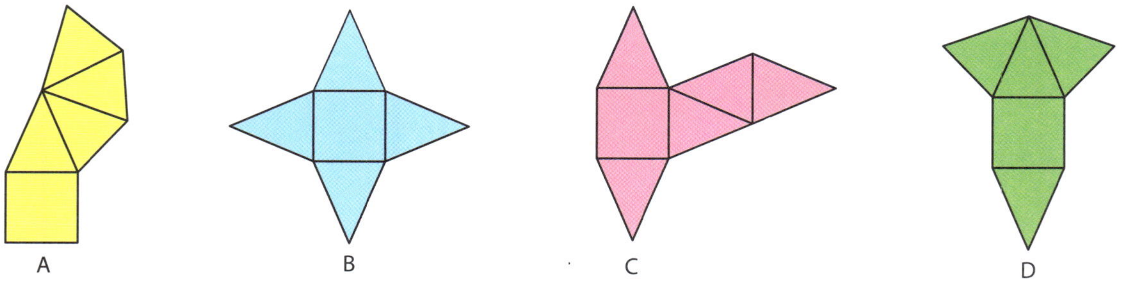

2 The opposite sides of 1 to 6 dice always add up to 7.

Here are the nets of some cubes or dice.

Add the missing numbers to the nets.

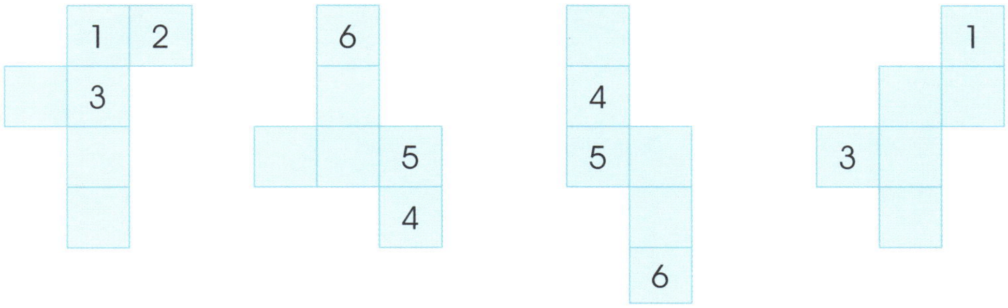

a) b) c) d)

3 Question 2 shows you four nets of a cube. There are 11 different nets for a cube.

Can you find the other 7 nets?

Be careful that the nets you find are not rotations or reflections of each other.

4 This is the net of pentagonal prism.

a) How many faces does a pentagonal prism have?

b) How many edges does a pentagonal prism have?

Hint: Remember some edges of the net will join and be the same edge.

c) How many vertices does a pentagonal prism have?

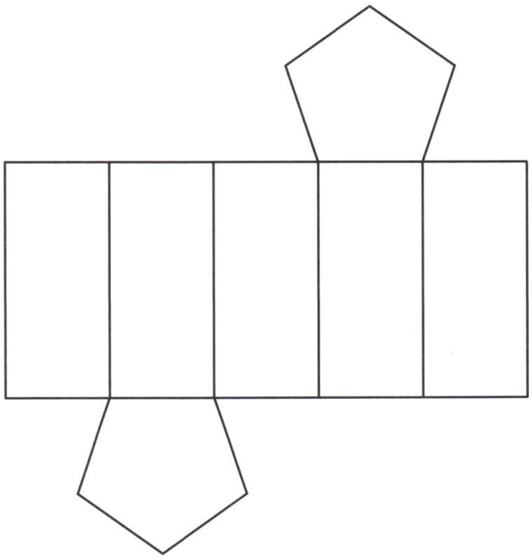

15 Co-ordinates and shapes

What will you learn?

How to:

- describe positions on the full coordinate grid (all four quadrants)
- construct, translate and reflect simple shapes on the co-ordinate plane, and reflect them in the axes.

I need to be able to:

- identify, describe and represent the position of a shape following a reflection or translation, using the appropriate language, and know that the shape has not changed.

Examples

1 Plot the points A (1, 4), B (2, 1) and C (4, 3) and join them to make an isosceles triangle. Write down the co-ordinates of the mid-point of the line BC.

2 Find the co-ordinates of a fourth point, D, so that ABCD is a parallelogram.

The mid-point of BC is (3, 2).

D is the point (3, 6). D could also be (5, 0) or (–1, 2)

(–1, 2) doesn't actually fit on this grid.

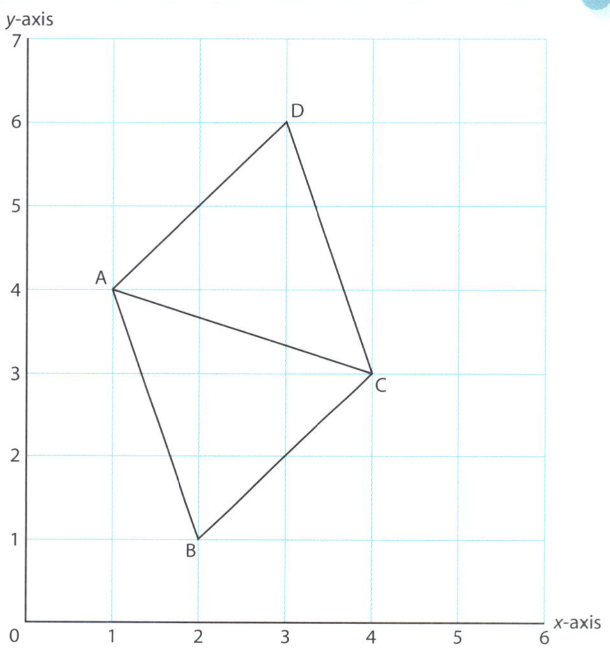

3 Reflect this pentagon in the y-axis.

- *Reflect means to 'flip over' or to show as it would appear in a mirror*

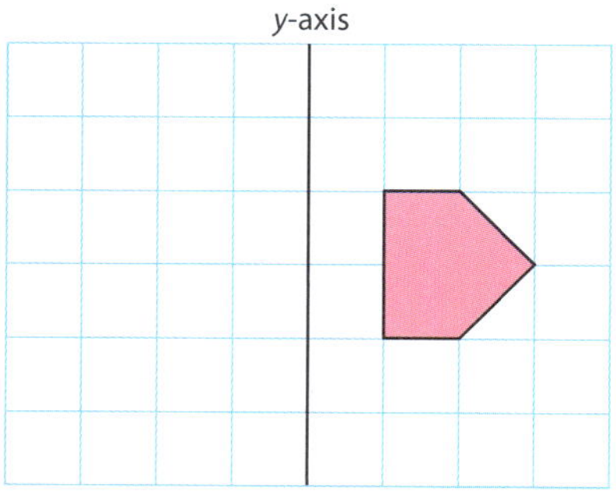

The original position

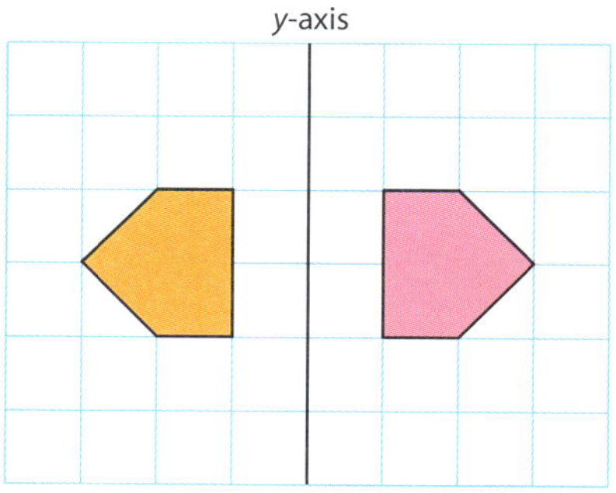

The pentagon has been 'flipped over'.

You need to check that:

- *The shape stays exactly the same distance from the mirror line.*
- *The shape stays exactly the same, but 'flipped over'.*

You may also be asked about the co-ordinates of the shape.

4 Translate this triangle one square right and one square up.

- *'Translate this shape' means 'move this shape'.*

The original position | The triangle has moved one unit (square) to the right. | The triangle has moved one unit up.

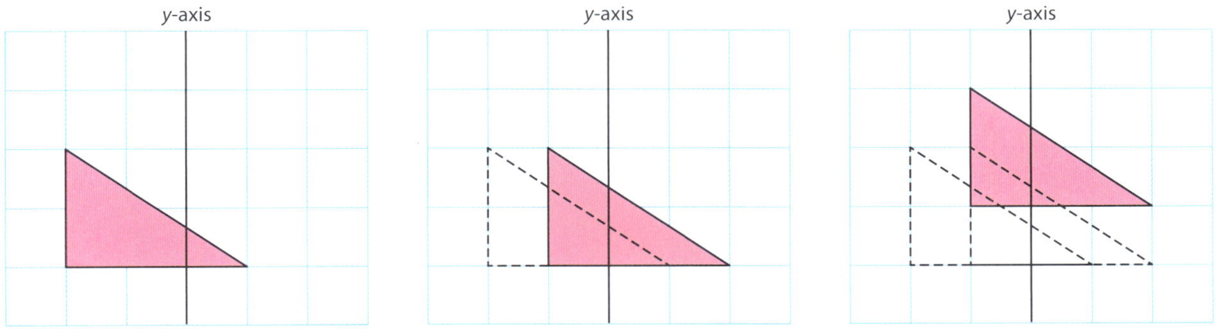

You need to check that:

- *Each vertex has moved the number of units or squares asked for in the question.*
- *The shape stays exactly the same.*

You may also be asked about the co-ordinates of the shape.

Translations to the right and up are described as positive numbers. Translations to the left and down are described as negative numbers. The translation above is described as (1,1).

Some grids use negative numbers in the x- and y-axes. This gives four sections to the grid; these are called the four quadrants.

Language

The x-axis goes across the grid, the y-axis goes up.
Co-ordinates are written as a pair of numbers with the x-value coming first.
E.g. a point with co-ordinates (5, 4) is 5 units across and 4 units up from (0, 0).

Language

Axis (plural **axes**) the line or lines on the grid that show the scale
Vertex (plural **vertices**) on a 3-D shape, a corner
Isosceles triangle a triangle with two equal sides
Reflection a 'flip over' movement in the mirror line
Translation a move to left or right and/or up and down, with no turning or 'flipping'

On track

1 Look at the grid. A and C are the two vertices of a square. X is the centre of the square.

Write down the co-ordinates of the other corners of the square.

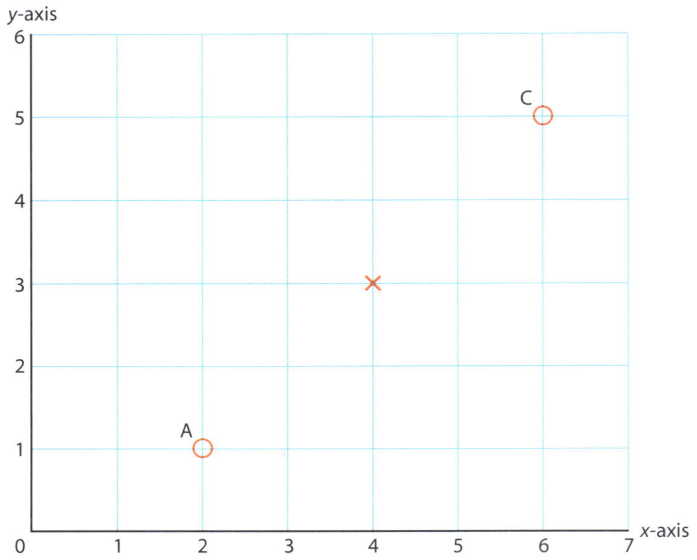

2 The shaded shape is a rectangle. Two of the co-ordinates are shown.

What are the co-ordinates of the two unmarked vertices?

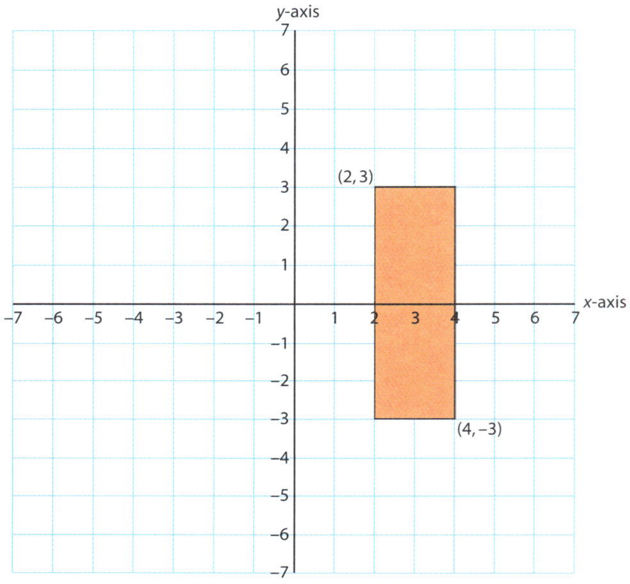

3 The co-ordinates of the square are shown.

Reflect the shape in the y-axis and give the four co-ordinates of its vertices.

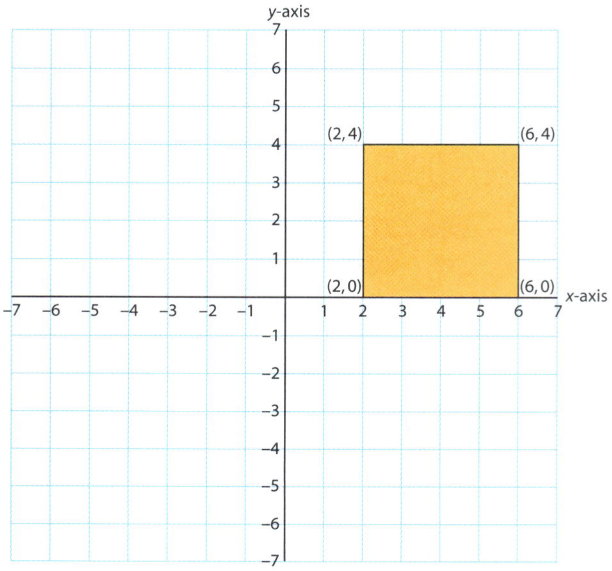

Aiming higher

1 Draw a co-ordinate grid on squared paper. Plot these points.

(2, 2) (6, 2) (10, 2) (6, 0) (6, 4) (4, 9) (8, 9)

Join them up in threes to make as many isosceles triangles as you can.

How many triangles have you found?

2 This triangle has been drawn on a grid.

a) What are its co-ordinates?

Translate vertex *a* (+8,0)

b) What will the new co-ordinates be?

(You can draw this on squared paper if you want.)

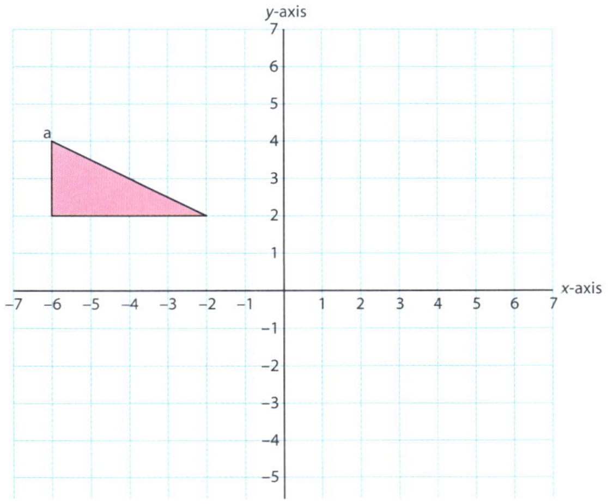

Using and applying

1 This right-angled triangle is translated down 2 units. Then it is reflected in the y-axis. What will its new co-ordinates be?

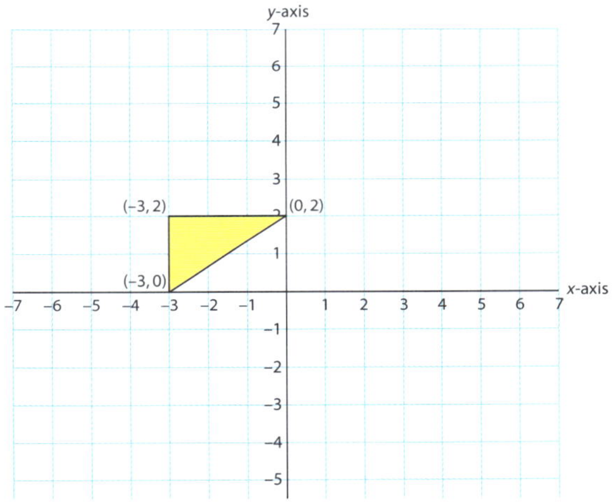

2 The co-ordinates shown are three vertices of a parallelogram.

By joining the points in different ways, it is possible to find three positions for the fourth vertex. What could the co-ordinates of the fourth vertex be?

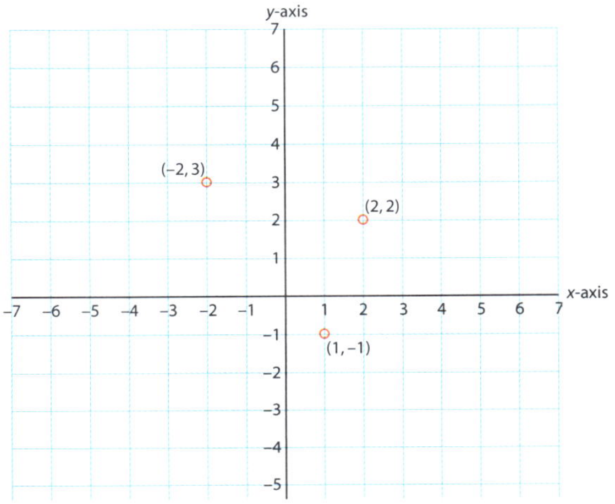

16 Measurement

What will you learn?

How to:

- use, read, write and convert between standard units, converting measurements of length, mass, volume and time from a smaller unit of measure to a larger unit and vice versa, including between miles and kilometres
- use decimal notation to three decimal places to solve problems involving calculation and conversion of measures.

I need to be able to:

- convert between different units of measure (e.g. kilometre and metre; metre and centimetre; centimetre and millimetre; kilogram and gram; litre and millilitre)
- understand and use basic equivalences between metric and common imperial units and express them in approximate terms.

Examples

1 Put these weights in order, smallest first.

1.275 kg   1500 g   160 g   2000 g   0.8 kg

First change weights into grams so all units are the same and can be compared:

$1.275\,kg = 1.275 \times 1000 = 1275\,g$, $0.8\,kg = 0.8 \times 1000 = 800\,g$.

The order is 160 g, 800 g, 1275 g, 1500 g, 2000 g.

Now write the weights using the original units:

160 g, 0.8 kg, 1.275 kg, 1500 g, 2000 g.

2 Change 5 inches into centimetres.

Every inch is about 2.5 cm, so multiply the number of inches by 2.5.

$5 \times 2.5 = 12.5$ *5 inches is about 12.5 cm.*

3 Change 15 miles into kilometres.

Every 5 miles is about 8 km, so divide the number of miles by 5 and multiply by 8

$15 \div 5 = 3$

$3 \times 8 = 24$ *so, 15 miles is about 24 km.*

4 Change 40 km into miles.

Every 8 km is about 5 miles, so divide the number of km by 8 and multiply by 5.

$40 \div 8 = 5$

$5 \times 5 = 25$ *so, 40 km is about 25 miles.*

Key facts

10 mm in 1 cm
100 cm in 1 m
1000 m in 1 km
1000 g in 1 kg
1000 ml in 1 litre

1 inch is about 2.5 cm.
5 miles is about 8 km.
1 kg is about 2.2 pounds.
1 litre is about $1\frac{3}{4}$ pints.
1 gallon is about $4\frac{1}{2}$ litres.

Language

centi ... in measurement means a hundredth
kilo ... in measurement means a thousand
milli ... in measurement means a thousandth

On track

1 a) Write these lengths in order, shortest first:

1.11 km   1010 m   1.011 km   1100 m

b) Write these lengths in order, shortest first:

5 m   555 cm   5005 mm   5.5 m   505 cm

c) Put these volumes in order, smallest first:

2 litres   1500 ml   1.6 litres   100 ml   0.75 litres

d) Put these weights in order, smallest first:

2 kg   1500 g   1.6 kg   10 000 g   34 kg

2 Milly has a 2 litre bottle of lemonade
She fills three cups that each hold 375 ml.
How much lemonade is left in the bottle?

Give your answer in a) millilitres b) litres.

3 Change these miles into kilometres:

a) 20 miles b) 40 miles c) 12.5 miles d) 100 miles

4 Change these kilometres into miles:

a) 64 kilometres b) 12 kilometres c) 80 kilometres d) 400 kilometres

5 How many minutes are there in:

a) 4 hours b) $2\frac{1}{2}$ hours c) $\frac{3}{4}$ hour? d) 1 day?

6 Change these 12-hour times to 24-hour times:

a) 11:50 am b) 3:15 pm c) 8:30 am d) 9:20 pm

7 Change these 24-hour times to 12-hour times:

a) 10:15 b) 17:05 c) 22:50 d) 06:00

Aiming higher

1 a) Change these lengths to centimetres:

2 m   3.5 m   20 mm   425 mm

b) Change these weights to grams:

2 kg   6.35 kg   0.525 kg   3.175 kg

c) Change these lengths to kilometres:

3865 m   5350 m   4005 m   75 m

2 A kilogram is about 2.2 pounds (lbs).

a) Change these weights into pounds (lbs):

6 kg   10 kg $\frac{1}{2}$ kg

b) Change these weights into kilograms:

4.4 lbs   11 lbs   44 lbs

3 A gallon is about $4\frac{1}{2}$ litres.

a) Change these litres into gallons:

9 litres   27 litres   45 litres

b) Change these gallons into litres:

3 gallons   7 gallons   20 gallons

4 a) What is quarter past 7 in the evening in 12-hour time?

b) What is half past 9 in the morning in 24-hour time?

5 This table gives the start time and end time of some films; it also tells you how long the film lasts. Fill in the missing sections.

	Start time	Duration	End time
a)	4:45 pm		7:10 pm
b)	5:05 pm	2 hours 35 minutes	
c)		3 hours 5 minutes	8:55 pm
d)	6:50 pm		9:40 pm
e)		2 hours 45 minutes	6:35 pm
f)	6:40 pm	2 hours 45 minutes	

Using and applying

1 Here is a signpost in a country park.

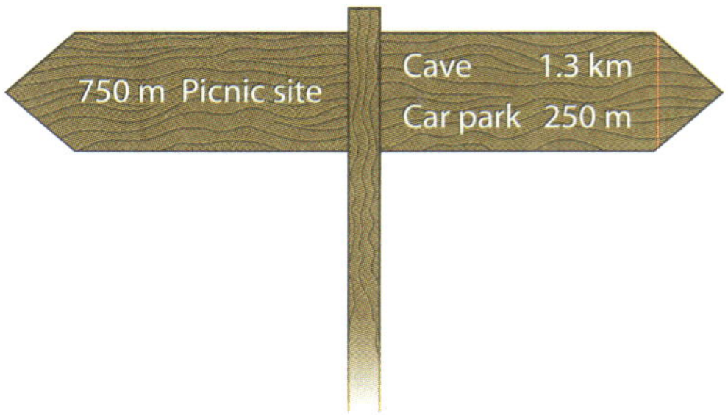

a) How much further is it to the cave than the car park?

b) Helen is at the cave. How far would she have to walk to the picnic site?

2 The distance from Ayton to Exton is **240 km**.

5 miles is approximately **8 km**.

Use this fact to calculate the approximate distance in **miles** from Ayton to Exton.

Show how you worked it out.

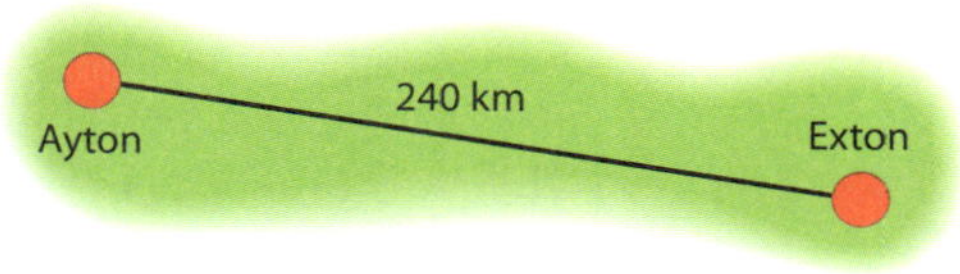

3 These are two distance charts. One chart is in miles and one is in kilometres.

Complete both charts.

Distance chart in miles

	London	New York	New Delhi	Tokyo
New York	3460			
New Delhi				
Tokyo	6955	11590		
Sydney		9945	6480	

Distance chart in kilometres

	London	New York	New Delhi	Tokyo
New York				
New Delhi	6696	11760		
Tokyo			5840	
Sydney	17000			4840

4 Here is a timetable for buses:

	BUSES				
	X45	**43**	**44**	**40**	**46**
Oak Green	10:35	11:05	11:25	11:50	12:10
Maple Street	10:45	11:15	11:35	12:00	12:20
Ash Terrace	10:49	11:21	11:39	12:06	12:30
Beech Drive				12:12	12:38
Poplar Close		11:37	11:46	12:17	
Elm Crescent	11:05		11:52	12:23	12:47

Answer these questions about the timetable:

a) How long does the X45 take to go from Oak Green to Elm Crescent?

b) Which bus does not go to Elm Crescent?

c) If I am at Oak Green at 10:55, waiting for a bus to Beech Drive:

i) Which bus will I get?

ii) How long will I have to wait for it?

iii) How long will my journey take?

17 Area and perimeter

What will you learn?

How to:

- recognise that shapes with the same areas can have different perimeters and vice versa
- calculate the area of parallelograms and triangles
- recognise when it is possible to use the formulae for area of shapes.

I need to be able to:

- measure and calculate the perimeter of composite rectilinear shapes in centimetres and metres
- calculate and compare the area of squares and rectangles including using standard units, square centimetres (cm^2) and square metres (m^2) and estimate the area of irregular shapes.

Examples

1 The area of a rectangle is $12\,cm^2$.

What are possible values for its length and width? What values of length and width give the smallest perimeter?

Area of a rectangle = length × width.

Using whole numbers only, what are the possible values for its length and width?

One number in each pair could be the length, the other the width.

Work out perimeters for each pair of numbers (2 × length + 2 × width):

1 and 12 gives 26 cm; 2 and 6 gives 16 cm; 3 and 4 gives 14 cm;

the smallest perimeter occurs when length = 4 cm and width = 3 cm.

2 Find the area of this triangle:

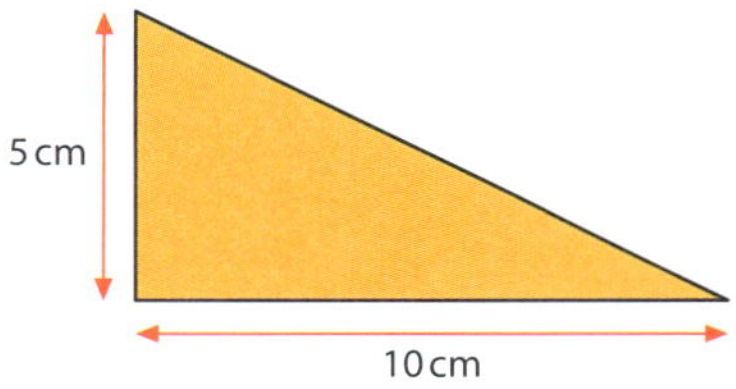

It's best to think of two triangles that are exactly the same.

If you flip the second triangle over, you can make a rectangle, which will be 10 cm × 5 cm

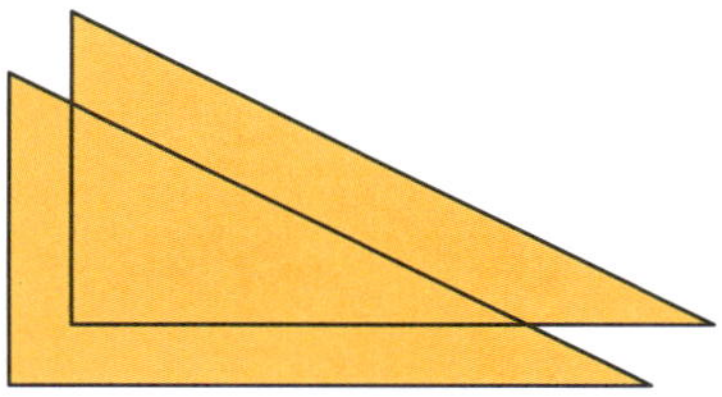

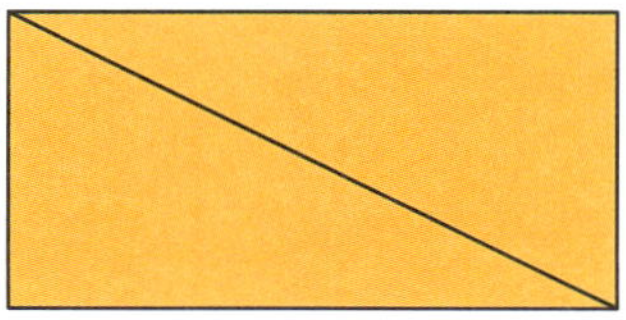

The area of the rectangle will be $10 \times 5 = 50$, so the area is 50 cm^2.

So you know that two identical triangles will also have an area of 50 cm^2, so each triangle must have an area of 25 cm^2.

To find the area of a triangle, you multiply the base of the triangle [the 10 cm part] by the height of the triangle [the 5 cm part] and halve the answer.

You might see this shortened into a formula in different ways:

$$A = b \times h \div 2 \qquad A = \tfrac{1}{2}bh \qquad A = \frac{bh}{2}$$

3 Find the area of this parallelogram:

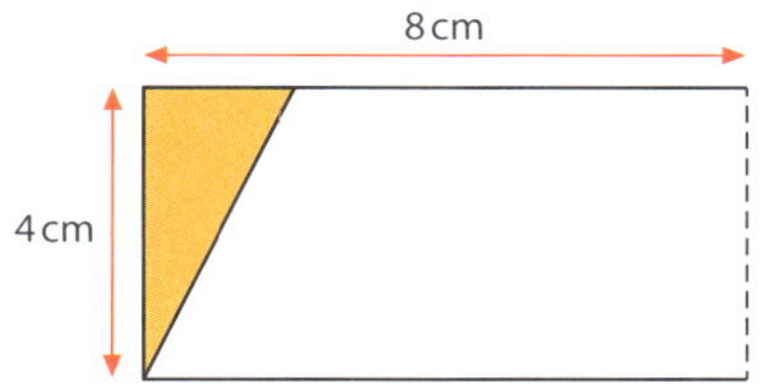

The 8 cm is the length of the parallelogram and the 4 cm is the height.

To find the area, you can divide the parallelogram into other shapes, like this:

By taking off the triangle on the right and adding it on to the left, you can make a rectangle. You know how to find the area of a rectangle.

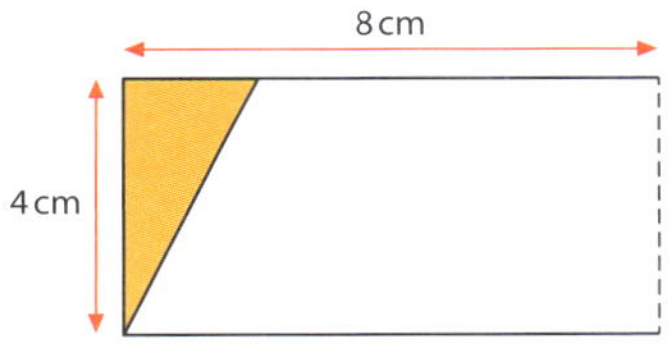

Length of the parallelogram × height of parallelogram

$8 \times 4 = 32$ cm^2

Key facts

Area is measured in square units, e.g. square centimetres (cm^2).
Perimeter is a length, so is measured in centimetres or metres or …

Useful area formulae:

Area of triangle $= \frac{1}{2} \times$ base $\times$ height
Area of parallelogram $=$ base $\times$ height

Language

Perimeter the distance around the edge of a flat shape

Area the amount of surface covered by the flat shape

On track

1 Find the area of the these triangles:

	base (cm)	height (cm)	area (cm^2)
a)	6	5	
b)	12	6	
c)	15	4	
d)	25	6	
e)	2.5	8	

2 Find the area of these parallelograms:

	base (cm)	height (cm)	area (cm^2)
a)	10	3	
b)	14	2	
c)	18	5	
d)	30	7	
e)	5.5	3	

3 Find the area of these triangles:

a)

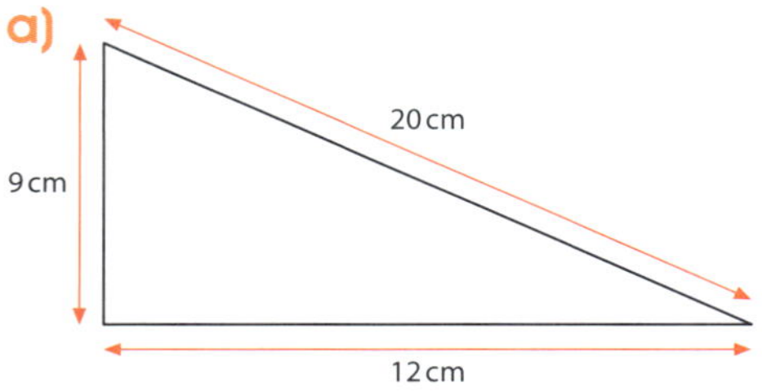

b)

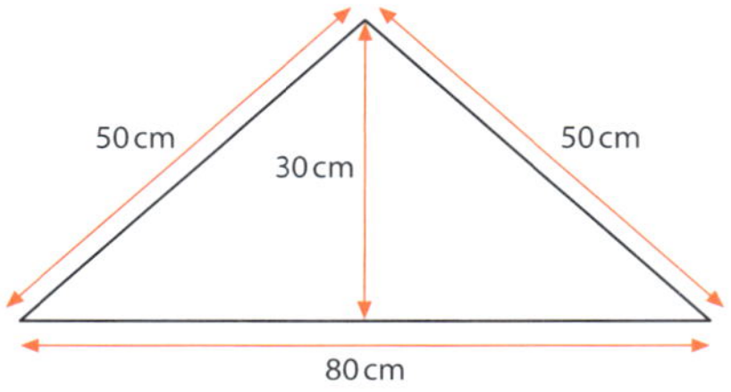

4 Find the area and perimeter of this parallelogram:

Aiming higher

1 The diagram shows a shaded square inside a large square.

a) Calculate the area of the large square.

b) Calculate the area of the smaller shaded square.

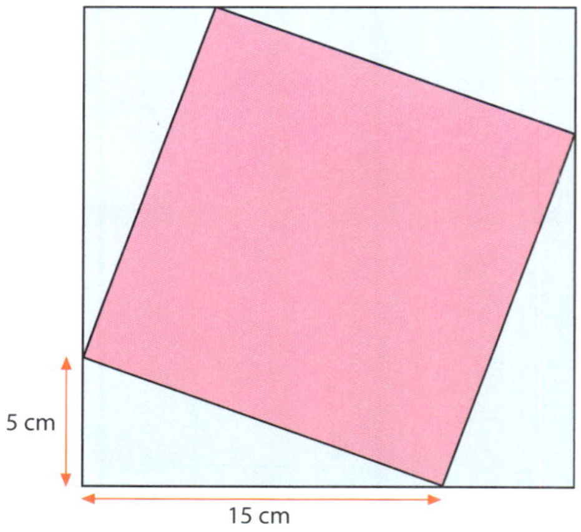

2 For these questions, give as many answers as possible using whole numbers only.

Hint: Think about the pairs of factors.

a) A rectangle has an area of 24 cm^2. What could its perimeter be?

b) A rectangle has an area of 36 cm^2. What could its perimeter be?

c) A rectangle has a perimeter of 20 cm. What could its area be?

d) A rectangle has a perimeter of 24 cm. What could its area be?

Hint: Remember to half the perimeter first.

3 What is the area of these shapes?

Hint: Divide the shapes into shapes of which you know how to find the area.

a)

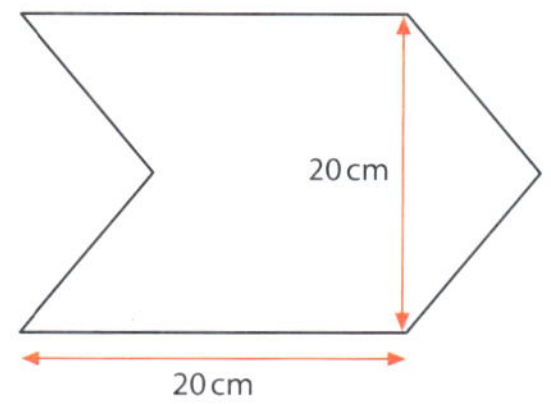

Extra hint: This shape is symmetrical.

b)

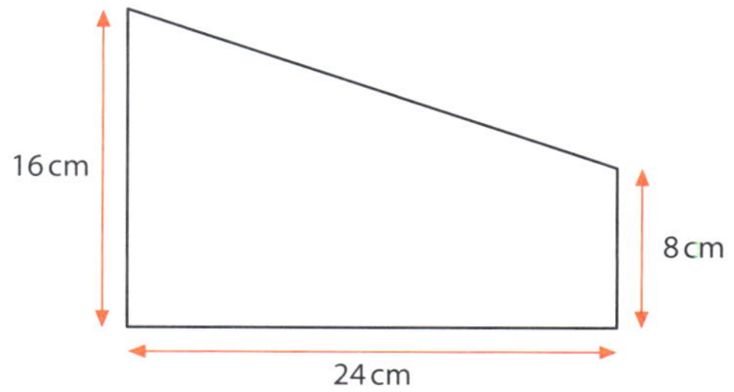

Using and applying

1 Here are some tiles. Each tile measures 4.5 cm by 6.5 cm.

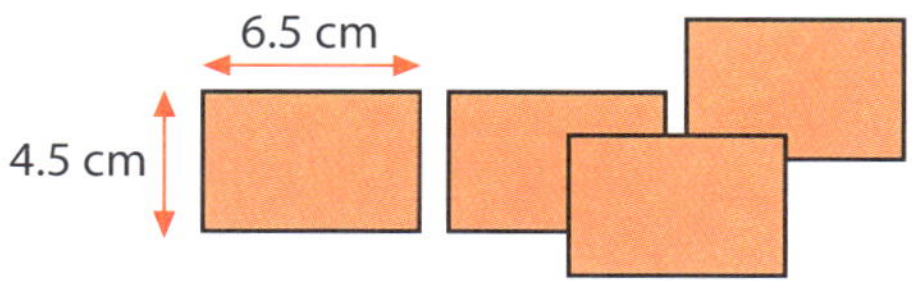

Michelle uses the tiles to cover the top of a rectangular table measuring 65 cm by 36 cm.

How many tiles does she need? Show how you worked it out.

2 A rectangle has a perimeter of 32 cm. One side measures 5 cm.

Calculate the area of the rectangle. Show your working.

3 The triangle ABC is an isosceles triangle.

The perimeter of the triangle is 56 cm.

The side AB is three times the length of the side AC.

What is the length of side AB?

4 On some centimetre squared paper, draw:

a) a parallelogram with an area of 28 cm^2

b) a triangle with an area of 12 cm^2

c) a square with a perimeter of 36 cm

d) a rectangle with a perimeter of 20 cm

5 You will need to use some centimetre squared paper.

a) Make some rectangles from twelve centimetre tiles or squares.

How many different perimeters can you find?

b) If you were asked to make some rectangles with an area of 12 cm^2, would the answers be different?

18 Volume

What will you learn?

How to:

- calculate, estimate and compare volume of cubes and cuboids using standard units including centimetre cubes (cm^3) and cubic metres (m^3), and extending to other units such as mm^3 and km^3
- recognise when it is possible to use the formulae for the volume of shapes.

I need to be able to:

- recognise and estimate volume (e.g. using $1 cm^3$ blocks to build cubes and cuboids) and capacity (e.g. using water).

Example

Find the volume of a cuboid 6 cm long, 3 cm broad and 2 cm high.

- *To record a volume, it is best to use a standard unit and it is usual to use cubes. These cubes are of a standard measure, such as centimetre cubes (cm^3) or metre cubes (m^3).*
- *To find the volume of the cuboid in the question, think about how many centimetre cubes would fit inside it.*

  There would be $6 cm^3$ along its length:

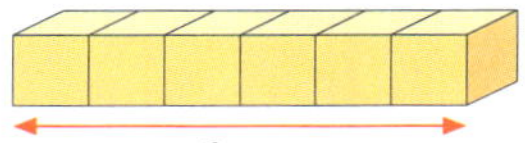

  There would be three rows of $6 cm^3$.

  $6 \times 3 = 18$, so there are $18 cm^3$ in this layer.

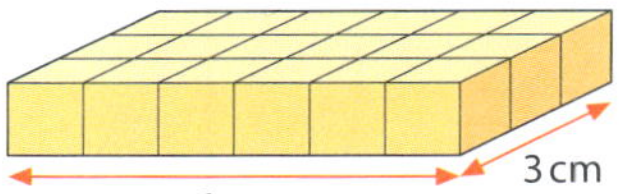

  There would be two layers of $18 cm^3$.

  $18 \times 2 = 36$, there are $36 cm^3$ in the cuboid.

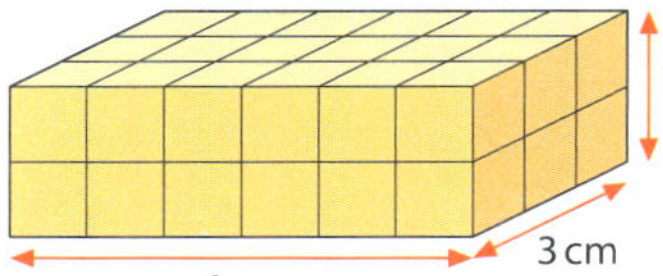

Key fact

To find the volume of a cuboid, multiply the length by the breadth by the height.
As a formula this is: $V = lbh$

Language

Volume the amount of space taken up by a 3-D solid or object, measured in mm^3, cm^3, m^3, km^3

Capacity the amount an object can hold, measured in millilitres (ml), centilitres (cl), litres (l)

On track

1 Find the volume of cubes that have these lengths:

a) 5 cm b) 8 cm c) 10 cm d) 20 cm e) 50 cm

2 A fish tank is 70 cm long, 40 cm broad and 40 cm high.

a) What is the volume of the fish tank?

b) If the tank is filled with water to 5 cm from the tank, what is the volume of the water?

Aiming higher

1 Find the volume of this cuboid.

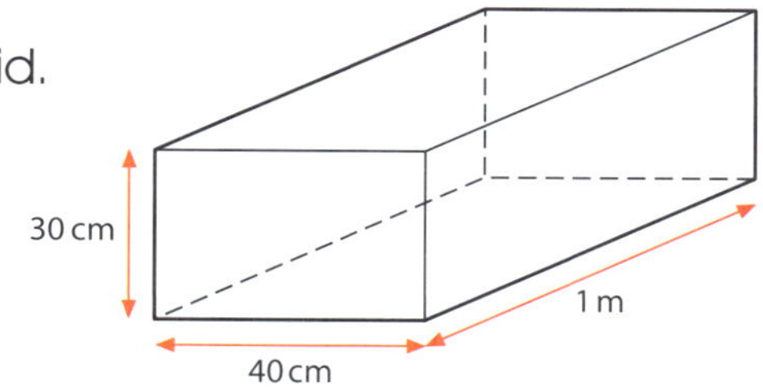

2 Find the volume of this cube.

Each face has an area of 16 cm^2.

Hint: Remember how to find the area of a square.

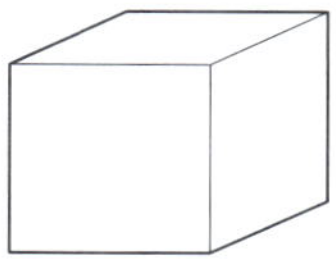

Using and applying

1 It's possible to find the volume of prisms by finding the area of the end face and multiplying by the length.

Find the volume of this triangular prism.

Hint: Remember how to find the area of a triangle; check unit 17 about area and perimeter.

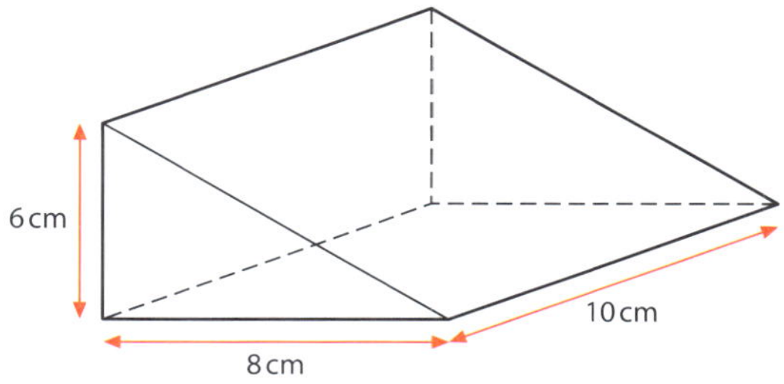

2 A cuboid has a volume of 36 cm^3.

What could the three dimensions of the cuboid be?

Find three possible answers.

19 Interpreting data

What will you learn?

How to:

- interpret, construct and use pie charts and line graphs and use these to solve problems.

I need to be able to:

- understand scales on axes and estimate points between marked labels.
- complete, read and interpret information in tables
- solve comparison, sum and difference problems using information presented in line graphs.

Examples

1 This line graph shows the temperature in a classroom from 08:00 to 18:00.
By how many degrees did the temperature increase from 08:00 to 16:00?

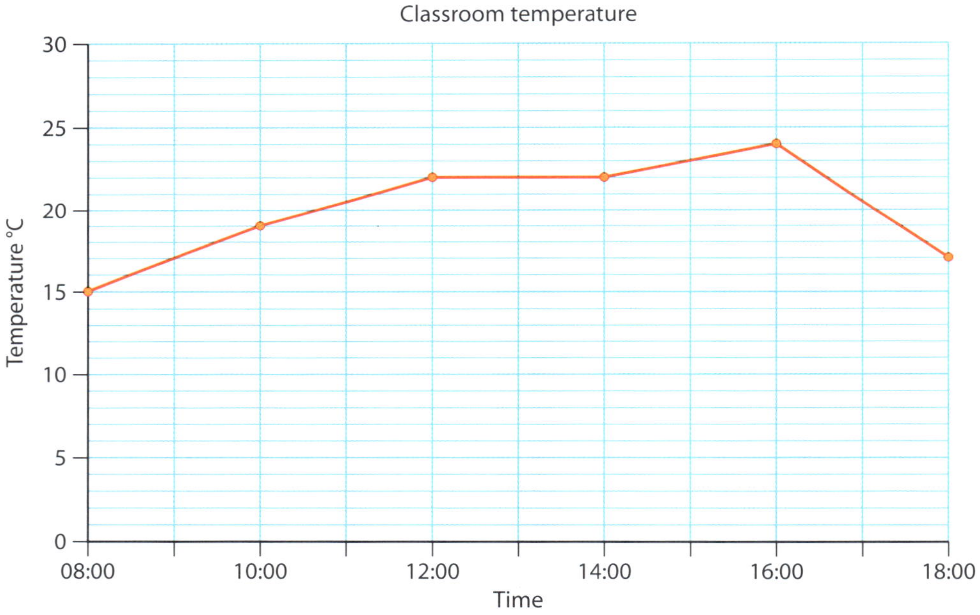

- *You need to find the temperatures for the two times.*

  Find 08:00 on the x-axis (the horizontal one). You do this by following the vertical line marking 08:00 until you reach the line of the line graph. Then read the temperature on the y-axis (the vertical one). It is 15°C.

  Now do the same for 16:00. It is 24°C.

  To answer the question, you need to find the difference between 15°C and 24°C.

  24 – 15 = 9, so the difference is 9°C.

A line graph shows continuous data. This means the data is changing: in the graph the temperature is changing over time. So you can use the graph opposite to find information between the labelled points.

- *Estimate the temperature at 08:30.*

  Using the same skills from earlier, 08:30 is a quarter of the way between 08:00 and 10:00. Going up to reach the line graph, and then moving horizontally, you can see the temperature at this time must have been about 16°C.

  It's important to remember that the line graph only gives an indication of the temperatures. The only temperature known for certain are those plotted and marked with the circular points.

2 This pie chart shows how children travel to school.

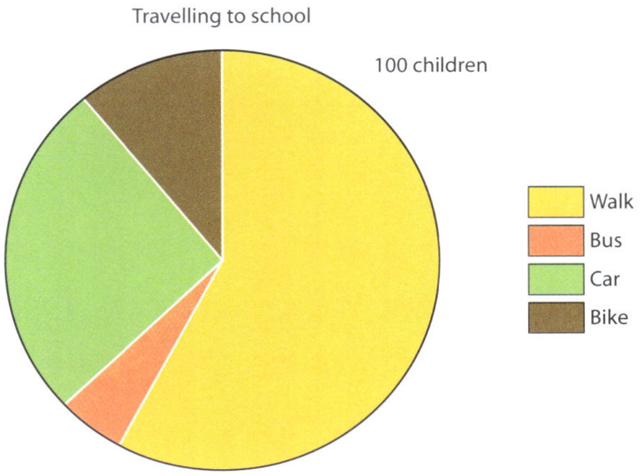

- Estimate the number of children who travelled to school by car.

  It's important to make sure you find the total value of the chart. This chart shows 100 children. Next, you need to look at each sector (piece of pie). For this question, you need to find the number of children who have travelled by car. The sector for 'car' is just over a quarter of the whole chart, so the number of children who travelled by car will be just over a quarter of 100. A good estimate would be 26.

  When you make pie charts the size of the sectors is based on 360°. To show a sector of 26 out of 100, or $\frac{26}{100}$, you need to find the value of $\frac{1}{100}$ as degrees ($360° \div 100 = 3.6$). So the sector for $\frac{26}{100}$ would be $26 \times 3.6 = 93.6°$.

Language

You must have equal intervals along each scale.
It does not always make sense to join up points in a line graph. Think carefully before you do it and consider the type of data you are using.

Language

Line graph a graph that uses lines to show how data may change in value as something changes; often how something changes over time

Continuous data data that can take any value in a range. It is measured rather than counted.

Pie chart a chart based on a circle. It is divided into sectors (pieces of pie) to show the relative values of the information.

On track

1 This line graph shows Karina's scores in weekly maths tests.

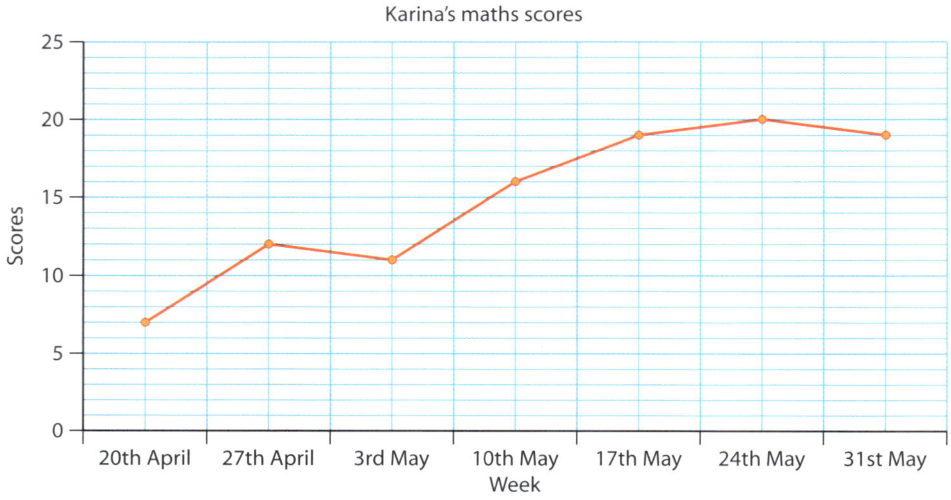

a) What was Karina's highest score?

b) What was Karina's lowest score?

c) What was the difference between Karina's highest and lowest scores?

2 At the end of the school year, children were asked what their favourite P.E. lesson had been. The results were shown in a pie chart.

a) How many children were asked about their favourite sport?

b) Which two sports were the same in popularity?

c) Estimate the number of children that liked tennis.

d) Which was the **least** popular sport?

e) Estimate how many more children liked netball than football.

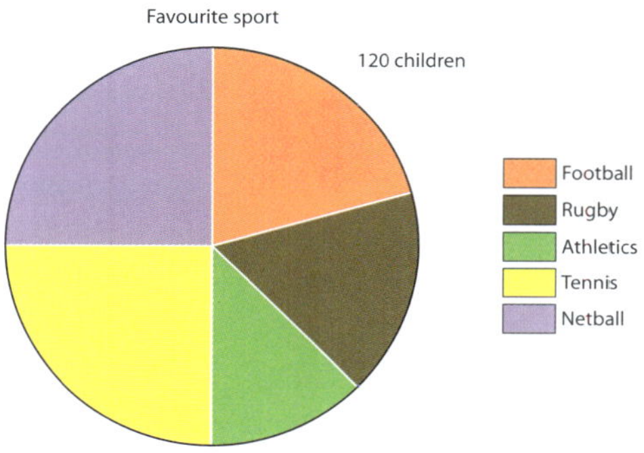

Aiming higher

1 This graph converts the temperature in degrees Celsius to degrees Fahrenheit.

a) Use the graph to change 30°C to °F.

b) Use the graph to change 140°F to °C.

c) The boiling point of water is 212°F. What is this in degrees Celsius?

d) The freezing point of water is 0°C. What is this in degrees Fahrenheit?

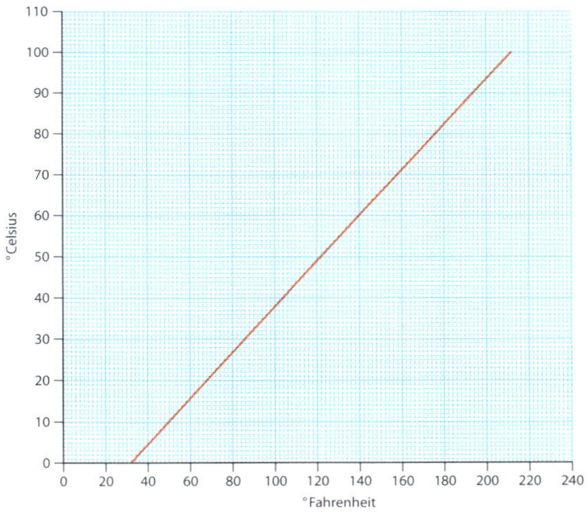

2 Two schools record what children do at lunch time: some have a school dinner, some bring a packed lunch and some go home. They record the results in pie charts.

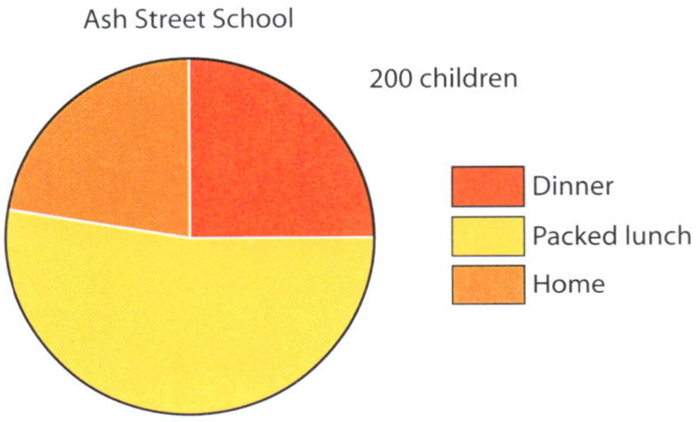

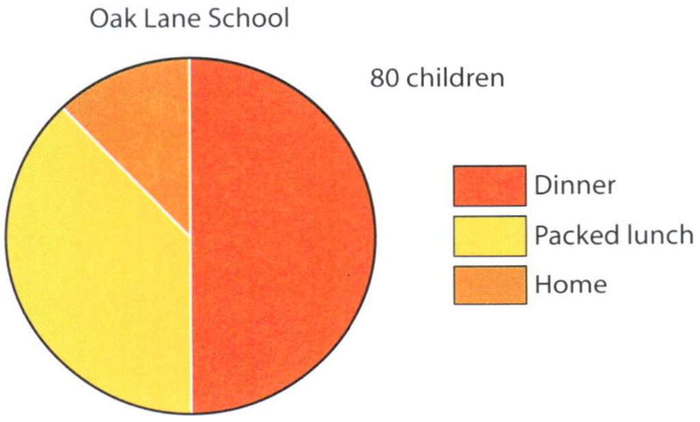

a) Which school had more children having a dinner? Give an estimate of the number having dinner in each school.

b) Estimate how many children had a packed lunch at:

i) Ash Street School

ii) Oak Lane School.

Using and applying

1 Ewan drew a pie chart to show the favourite sandwiches in 120 children's packed lunches. These are the sizes he drew for each sector.

How many children chose each type of sandwich as their favourite?

Sandwiches	Size of angle
Beef	15°
Chicken	45°
Cheese	105°
Ham	84°
Prawn	6°
Tuna	69°
Salad	36°

20 Averages – Mean

What will you learn?

How to:

- calculate and interpret the mean as an average.

I need to be able to:

- add and divide numbers
- solve problems.

Examples

Children in Year 6 had an English test. Their marks were: 90, 65, 85, 100, 75, 95, 80, 75, 70.

1 What was the mean mark?

*The **mean** mark is found by:*

adding together all the marks:

90 + 65 + 85 + 100 + 75 + 95 + 80 + 75 + 70 = 735

and then dividing by the number of marks:

*735 ÷ 9 = 81.67, so the **mean** = 81.67 or 82 to the nearest whole mark.*

The mean time spent doing homework by a group of 14 children is 55 minutes.

2 What was the total time spent by all 14 children doing their homework?

The mean time taken by each children is 55 minutes, so the total time must be 55 × 14 = 770. This is 770 minutes or 12 hours 50 minutes.

A fifteenth child is added to the group. He spent 1 hour and 40 minutes doing his homework.

3 What will the new mean time be?

From the previous question, you know that the total time for 14 children is 770 minutes. The fifteenth child will add 100 minutes (1 hour 40 minutes) to the total.

770 + 100 = 870

The total need to be divided by 15.

870 ÷ 15 = 58

The new mean is 58 minutes.

Key fact

The mean of a set of data is found by adding the data and dividing the total by the number of data.

Language

The **mean** is sometimes just called the average.

On track

1 Linford runs 100m eight times. These are his times in seconds:

13.5   14.1   13.5   13.2   14.1   13.8   13.4

What is his mean (average) time?

2 Write three different numbers so that the mean of the three numbers is 12.

3 The mean of four numbers is 5.

Three of the numbers are 2, 3 and 8.

What is the fourth?

Aiming higher

1 The mean of eight numbers is 16.

A ninth number is added and the new mean is 20.

What is the value of the ninth number?

2 The mean of seven numbers is 122.

One number, 146, is taken away from the group.

What will the new mean be?

3 A, B and C stand for three different numbers.

The mean of A and B is 50. The mean of A and C is 45. A + B + C = 150

Calculate the values of A, B and C.

Using and applying

1 Here are set of number cards.

Two of the cards are face down.

The mean of the seven numbers is 17.

What could the two hidden numbers be?

2 Here are four numbers cards, all face down.

The mean of the four cards is 15. What could the four numbers be?

Glossary

Area the amount of surface covered by the flat shape

Cancel divide both numbers in a fraction by the same factor

Capacity the amount an object can hold

Circumference the distance around the outside of a circle

Common factor a factor which is a factor of two numbers

Common multiple a number that is a multiple of at least two numbers

Continuous data data that can take any value in a range. It is measured rather than counted

Denominator the bottom number of a fraction

Diameter the shortest distance through the centre of a circle joining two opposite points on the edge of the circle

Equation a mathematical sentence that uses symbols (=) to say two things are of the same value

Factor a number that divides exactly into another

Formula numbers and symbols used as instructions to solve a calculation

Integers whole numbers

Multiple a number in another number's times table

Net the faces of a 3-D solid opened out and laid flat

Numerator the top number of a fraction

Parallel faces remain the same distance apart along all of their dimensions

Perimeter the distance around the edge of a flat shape

Perpendicular faces are at right angles to each other

Prime number has only two factors – itself and 1

Product the number found by multiplying two numbers together

Proportion compares a part to the whole

Radius the shortest distance from the centre of a circle to the edge

Ratio compares a part to a part

Reflection a 'flip over' movement in the mirror line

Side a line joining two vertices on a 2-D shape

Substitute replacing letters in formulae and equations with numbers

Translation a move to left or right and/or up and down, with no turning or 'flipping'

Vertex (plural vertices) a corner on a 2-D shape

Volume the amount of space taken up by a 3-D solid or object